RIGHTLY DIVIDING *the* WORD *of* TRUTH

SHARI S. ABBOTT

Study to show thyself approved unto God, a workman that needeth not to be ashamed, rightly dividing the word of truth.

—2 Timothy 2:15

All Scripture is given by inspiration of God, and is profitable for doctrine, for reproof, for correction, for instruction in righteousness.

—2 Timothy 3:16

RIGHTLY DIVIDING *the* WORD *of* TRUTH

That I may publish with the voice of thanksgiving, and tell of all thy wondrous works. (Psalm 26:7)

Published by Psalm 267 Publishing
www.psalm267.com | info@psalm267.com

Cover Design by Jackson C. Delany.

All emphasis and bracketed information added.

Printed in the United States of America
ISBN: 978-1-7361076-5-2

RIGHTLY DIVIDING *the* WORD *of* TRUTH

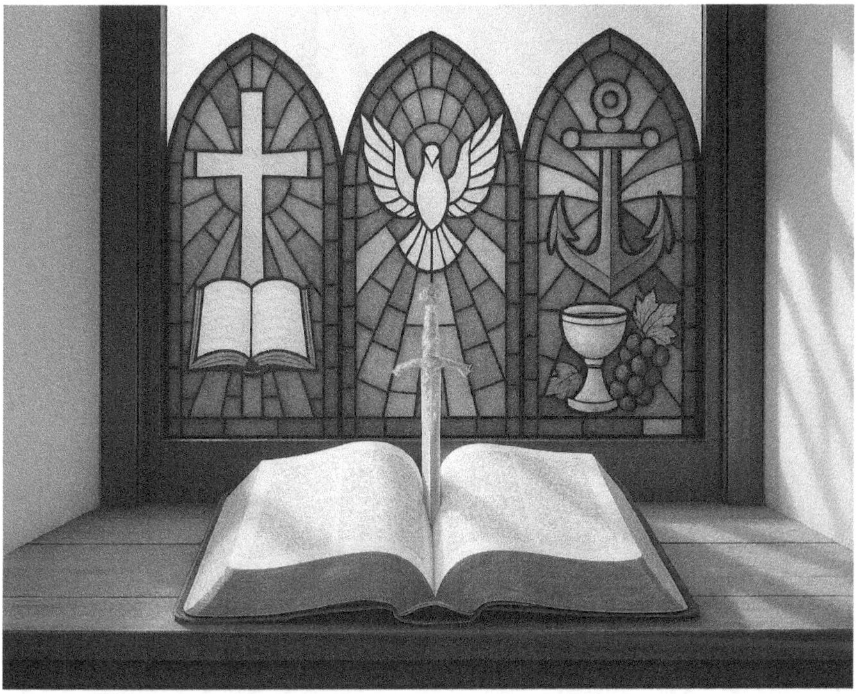

Contents

"Timothy was to divide rightly the word of God. This every Christian minister must do if he would make full proof of his ministry. The word of truth has to be taken to pieces wisely; it is not to be hacked or torn as by a wild beast, but rightly divided."

— Charles H. Spurgeon (1834-1892)

Foreword

> *"Study to show thyself approved unto God, a workman that needeth not to be ashamed, rightly dividing the word of truth." (2 Timothy 2:15)*

Such a simple verse. Yet even though I grew up an avid Bible reader and consider myself a capable Bible teacher, I did not always understand what Paul meant by "rightly dividing." One day, my dear friend Tad, who had spent countless hours in my Bible studies, pulled me aside and asked me to reflect more deeply on the apostle Paul's counsel. Over the years, as he listened and watched my teaching, he sensed that beneath my confident exterior—my pride in knowing Scripture and my joy in counting myself among the saved—stood a troubled soul. He recognized that there were still parts of God's Word I found hard to explain or reconcile, but I did not want to admit that. He understood that this struggle was keeping me from fully experiencing the liberty of grace through faith in Christ Jesus.

I vividly remember the specific conflict that weighed on me then. It was a distant but constant nagging I had tried to ignore for as long as I could remember. My inescapable, deeply hidden spiritual fear was the thought of someday standing before My Savior and giving an account of my life. I thought I knew grace. I believed I understood the forgiveness of the cross and what it meant to be washed in the blood of the Lamb. Yet I was constantly troubled by thoughts of being judged "according to my works," as Paul described in Romans and John prophesied of in Revelation.

My friend somehow sensed that my inescapable fear was my realization that my life could never withstand such scrutiny—that any judgment of my works would expose me as the fraud I felt myself to be. He also reasoned that the root of this fear lay in my lack of understanding about how to rightly divide the Word of Truth. At the time, I had no idea that was the key to reconciling Paul's description of the Judgment Seat of Christ and John's prophecy about the Great White Throne judgment.

Now I suspect that many readers of this book are in the same place as I once was. You love the Scriptures, you believe God and trust Him, yet at times the Bible still feels confusing. Take heart—I believe a whole new world is about to open to you through this book and its careful, thoughtful presentation by a skilled author, Shari Abbott.

As you read, you will soon learn that "rightly dividing" calls us to make careful distinctions about time, place, speaker, and audience as the Bible takes us on a six-thousand-year journey of progressive revelation unveiled by God.

Many of us have been taught that ALL of the Bible was written directly to us in the Church and that there are no so-called "distinctions" in Scripture to be made. But consider whether God has designed anything in life to work that way. Everything worth knowing or important to discover is built on discernment gained through recognizing distinctions.

My vocational career was spent in the medical field, where fine distinctions underlie accurate diagnoses and are critical to correct selection among an endless array of treatment options essential to good outcomes. What is learned about one individual, or about groups of similar people, if applied without distinction to all others, would lead to misdiagnoses and treatment options that prove tragic for some.

I cannot emphasize enough why and how the subject of this book matters so greatly to all of us in the Body of Christ. At a time when biblical knowledge is declining and doctrinal confusion is increasing, we need Christians to read and use the Bible the way God intends—so their faith is strong, their walk is steady, and their witness is clear.

Foreword

I have known Shari Abbott as a fellow Bible teacher, an expert Christian apologist, a talented author, and a close friend for many years. I know as well as anyone how seriously she takes her labor for the Lord. In 2011, God called her into a full-time apologetics ministry to help believers move from "I know this is true, but I don't quite understand it" to "I see how this fits, and I can explain it to someone else." The mission of her ministry is simple and needed: to equip Christians with knowledge, encourage them with understanding, and empower them to share Jesus with others.

One thing that stands out about Shari's work is her commitment to clarity. She wants rightly dividing to be both understandable and attainable for everyday believers. By walking through the basic distinctions God has built into His Word, Shari shows how rightly dividing protects us from error and opens our eyes to the beauty of God's plan and purposes.

This book is simple enough for a new reader of Scripture and a helpful refresher for those who have studied the Bible for years. While other books on this topic may depend on complex charts and lots of details, this one focuses on helping you internalize a basic framework you can actually use.

As you read the chapters of *Rightly Dividing the Word of Truth*, I encourage you not to rush. Take your time and read this book with an open Bible. Look up the verses and ponder God's words, using the tools of rightly dividing to become a better workman and to understand the verses in context. Understand that rightly dividing is not just a phrase; it is a skill.—and like any worthwhile skill, it grows stronger with use.

It is my sincere joy to commend this book, its author, and the Reasons for Hope* Jesus ministry to you. My prayer is that, through these pages, the Holy Spirit will sharpen your understanding, strengthen your faith, steady your daily walk, and deepen your love for our Lord Jesus Christ.

May you finish this book not only with a clearer approach to studying the Bible, but also more in awe of the God who has spoken, and more eager to be an unashamed workman—rightly dividing the Word of Truth.

Scott Hamlin

Retired CFO and COO, Cincinnati Children's Hospital
Servant and Unashamed Workman for Christ Jesus

Introduction

For countless Christians, the Bible is a source of profound inspiration, comfort, and truth. Yet, many also confess to finding it to be a confusing book, and at times, to be contradictory. After all, it's not a single volume but rather a library of 66 distinct books, written over 1,500 years by 40 different authors from every walk of life—from kings and scholars to fishermen and shepherds. The pages of the Bible contain a vast array of literary styles, including history, law, poetry, and prophecy, each with its own rules of interpretation, and with many literary devices that must be understood.

Why must we rightly divide the Word of God?

How does a believer today make sense of all the Bible has to say? How do we reconcile a command given to ancient Israel with an instruction given to the early Church? How do we distinguish a promise for a future kingdom from a principle for our present lives? Without a reliable method for navigating this divine library, readers can easily become lost, misapply verses, and draw confusing conclusions. This confusion can create doubt and foster doctrinal error. It can even cause believers to shy away from large portions of Scripture, considering them irrelevant or finding them incomprehensible.

The Bible itself provides the key. In his final letter to his beloved apprentice, Timothy, the Apostle Paul issues a charge that is as relevant today as it was in the first century:

> *"Study to show thyself approved unto God, a workman that needeth not to be ashamed, rightly dividing the word of truth." (2 Timothy 2:15)*

This command reveals that God doesn't want His children to be confused by His Word. He has provided a path to clarity.

"Rightly dividing" is a translation of the Greek word, orthotomeō, which conveys the image of a craftsman making a precise and straight cut. It is the skill of a stonemason ensuring a perfect fit, a farmer plowing a straight furrow, or a carpenter building a structure that is true and sound. In the same way, the student of the Bible is called to be a skilled workman, handling God's Word with the care and precision it deserves. We'll discuss this further in chapter one.

Why is rightly dividing so important?

Rightly dividing is the difference between confusion and clarity. It is the key that unlocks the beautiful, consistent, and progressive story of God's plan for the ages. It allows us to understand who is speaking, to whom they are speaking, and in what context. It protects us from the danger of claiming promises that were never made to us or taking on burdens we were never meant to carry. Failure to rightly divide can lead to serious doctrinal error, as Paul himself warned in the verses that follow his directive to rightly divide.

The Purpose of this Book

I have written this book for every Christian who desires to move from being a sometimes-confused reader to a confident workman. It is a guide for those who want to understand not just what the Bible says, but what it really means—for the original audience and for us today. It will equip you with the foundational principles and practical tools to "cut straight," to discern the vital distinctions God has placed within His Word, and to see the magnificent tapestry He has woven from Genesis to Revelation.

The reward for this labor is a faith built on solid ground, an unshakable assurance in God's promises, a deeper, more intimate communion with the Author Himself, and a confidence to share your faith.

As you read this book, you'll find repetition. First, a definition of key understandings for rightly dividing and then a "digging deeper" for a clearer understanding and to reinforce the concepts. We all learn well and remember better by repetition, so understand that concepts repeated will be concepts remembered.

The "-ologies" of Systematic Theology

One thing to keep in mind as we approach rightly dividing is to begin with an understanding of Systematic Theology. Systematic Theology is defined as the organized study and presentation of biblical doctrines by arranging theological topics into logical categories ("-ologies") to create a comprehensive and coherent understanding of the Christian faith.

Each "-ology" is a distinctive doctrine:

Theology Proper—the study of the doctrine of God.

Paterology—the study of God the Father.

Bibliology—the study of the Bible.

Christology—the study of Jesus.

Pneumatology—the study of the Holy Spirit.

Angelology—the study of the angelic beings, fallen and unfallen.

Anthropology— the study of humanity.

Soteriology—the study of Salvation.

Ecclesiology—the study of the Church.

Israelology—the study of Israel.

Eschatology—the study of last things or end times.

We will not address each of these "-ologies" in this book, but all are worthy of individual study. Even a basic knowledge will help in rightly dividing and rightly applying what the Bible says.

Covenant, Reformed, and Dispensational Theologies

We would be remiss if we left this section without addressing Covenant, Reformed, and Dispensational Theology.

- Covenant Theology is a biblical and hermeneutical framework for reading and understanding the Bible through the lens of God's covenants with humanity, especially the Adamic, Noahic, Abrahamic, Mosaic, Davidic, and New Covenant, as well as through three theological covenants—the Covenants of Redemption, Works, and Grace. Understanding the Covenants is important, but how we understand them differs through the lenses of Reformed and Dispensational Theology—distinct "camps" within the church that have differing views about Israel and the Church, biblical interpretation, and eschatology (end times).
- Reformed Theology emphasizes the unity of God's people throughout history and a continuity between Israel and the Church, with the Church inheriting and fulfilling the promises to Israel. It has a more typological (and allegorical) approach to Scripture. And when it comes to the end times, Reformed Theology sees the Church as the spiritual continuation of the Old Testament people of God.
- Dispensational Theology, in contrast, views a significant distinction between Israel and the Church, defining them as two distinct people groups under different covenants and with separate destinies. It approaches Scripture with literal interpretation, especially for Old Testament prophecies concerning Israel's future. And it understands Scripture to teach a distinct future national and literal kingdom for Israel after a yet future rapture of the Church and world-wide seven year tribulation.

Dispensational Theology is also called Dispensationalism, and it is the theology upon which rightly dividing is built. While the word "dispensation" is often thought to refer to time periods, the

Greek word actually carries a meaning defined by God's relationship and work with humanity. The Greek word "oikonomia" means: administration (of a household or estate); spec. a (religious) "economy"-- stewardship.

Rightly Dividing Made Simple

There are many books about rightly dividing, but most are lengthy, in-depth, technical, and intimidating. This book has a different goal: it is not to be comprehensive but instead to be comprehensible—that is, to make the essentials clear and give a concise overview of the key principles that will help you quickly learn how to read and study the Bible.

Be sure to use the pages at the back of the book. They're designed for your notes as you read—jot down insights you want to remember, verses to revisit, and questions you want to explore further.

Now, let's jump in and begin the journey to becoming an unashamed workman, rightly dividing the Word of Truth.

Chapter 1

What Does "Rightly Dividing" Mean?

Let's begin by breaking down the foundational command given by the Apostle Paul to his young protégé, Timothy. This single verse serves as our blueprint, our divine mandate for how we should approach the Word of God:

> *"Study to show thyself approved unto God, a workman that needeth not to be ashamed, rightly dividing the word of truth." (2 Timothy 2:15)*

This charge is not merely a suggestion; it is a command packed with profound implications for every believer. It speaks of a specific attitude (study), a noble identity (a workman), and an essential method (rightly dividing).

Let's explore each of these components to fully grasp the significance of handling God's Word correctly.

Study! The Attitude of a Devoted Heart

We all understand the word "study." From our earliest school days, we know it involves focus, repetition, and a desire to gain knowledge and understanding. The Greek word for study is "spoudazo," which means "to make an effort, be prompt or earnest, give diligence, be diligent, endeavor, labor, or study." In Ephesians 4:3, this word is translated as "endeavoring;" in Hebrews 4:11, it appears as "labor" (KJV) or "be diligent" (NKJV, et al.); in 2 Peter 1:10, it is "give diligence"; and in 2 Peter 3:14, it is "be diligent."

Therefore, this is not merely a command to study as an academic exercise. It suggests a dedicated effort and labor; however, the work of studying the Bible should always be a labor of love.

While the verse suggests that our studying will show us "approved unto God," we must remember that in Christ, we are already fully and eternally approved. We are positionally secure in our union with Him through His finished work.

The command to study to be approved is practical. It aims for us to experience more fully the grace we have received, to live more in accordance with God's will and ways, and thereby to please God. By dedicating our time and mental energy to studying the Bible, we demonstrate the value we place on God and His words. This act of devotion reflects our desire to know Him more intimately. It deepens our communion with Him by growing our knowledge of His character, will, and ways. This kind of study transforms the heart, renews the mind, and aligns our thoughts with His.

A Workman Who Needeth Not Be Ashamed

Paul doesn't call Timothy a philosopher, a debater, or even just a reader. He calls him a workman. Being a workman is an honorable calling and a metaphor rich in meaning. A good workman is diligent, precise, and respects his craft. He doesn't show up to the job site and handle his tools carelessly. He knows that sloppy work leads to unstable structures and that imprecise cuts can ruin the entire project. He takes pride in his labor, desiring that the final product be sound, accurate, and pleasing to the one who commissioned it.

In the same way, the student of the Bible is a spiritual craftsman. The "word of truth" is our sacred material, and the principles of right division are our tools. Our goal is to build a strong, stable faith—first in our own lives, and then in the lives of those we influence. A workman who "needeth not to be ashamed" handles the Word with such integrity and care that he can stand before God, his Master Builder, with confidence. He has not twisted Scripture for his own ends, taken verses out of context, or constructed a shaky theological system from crooked interpretations. His work is sound, and he has no reason to be ashamed.

Rightly Dividing! The Method for Precision

Those two words—rightly and dividing—together are the key that unlocks the entire process. As mentioned in the introduction, the Greek word orthotomeō, literally means "to cut straight" and paints the vivid picture of a craftsman performing his task with skill and precision. .

- It's the action of a carpenter snapping a chalk line to ensure a perfectly straight cut.
- It's the work of a stonemason chiseling a block so it fits flawlessly into place.
- It's the path of a farmer plowing a furrow that is straight and true, ensuring a good and orderly crop.
- It's the care of a steward faithfully dispensing the correct portions of food to the household at the proper time.

A workman who "cuts straight" produces quality work that is valuable, useful, and beautiful. The same is true when we "cut straight" the Word of God. By making the proper distinctions and divisions that are already present in the text, we arrive at a precise understanding, free from misinterpretations and misapplications. With better understanding comes correct application. When we apply God's Word correctly, our own souls are blessed, we become equipped to edify others, and, most importantly, we glorify the God of all truth.

The Danger of Not Rightly Dividing

If rightly dividing brings clarity and confidence, then the failure to do so inevitably leads to confusion, doctrinal error, and a distorted view of God. Paul doesn't leave this to our imagination. Immediately following his charge to Timothy, he provides a sobering, real-world example of the damage done by workmen who cut crooked.

> *"But shun profane and vain babblings: for they will increase unto more ungodliness. And their word will eat as doth a canker [gangrene]: of whom is Hymenaeus and Philetus; Who concerning the truth have erred, saying that the resurrection is past already; and overthrow the faith of some." (2 Timothy 2:16-18)*

Paul's warning is severe. The teaching of these men, Hymenaeus and Philetus, was not a minor disagreement. It was a spiritual gangrene that was corrupting healthy tissue and "overthrowing the faith of some." Their core error was a direct failure to rightly divide God's timeline concerning the resurrection. Influenced by an early form of Gnosticism that viewed all physical matter as evil, they spiritualized the resurrection, claiming it was a purely symbolic event that happened at conversion. They failed to "cut straight" between the present reality of spiritual life in Christ and the future physical reality of the bodily resurrection of believers unto glorification.

This single error had catastrophic consequences. First, it stripped believers of their "blessed hope"—the promise of a future, physical resurrection, which is the cornerstone of the Christian faith (1 Corinthians 15). Second, by denying a future judgment and bodily resurrection, it opened the door to lawlessness. If the body doesn't matter and resurrection is already past, then what one does in the flesh becomes irrelevant.

The story of Hymenaeus and Philetus is a permanent warning embedded in Scripture. It proves that handling the Word of Truth is a high-stakes calling. A sloppy workman can cause a building to collapse; a sloppy theologian can cause a person's faith to be crushed. Therefore, Paul so strongly urges Timothy—and us—to be diligent workmen who study and master the skill of rightly dividing the Word of Truth. It is the one of the most important safeguards against the dangers of false doctrine.

<*}}}><

Chapter 2

Two Rules for the Workman

The Bible is a perfectly unified book, authored by one divine author—the Holy Spirit. It was given to humanity through many human writers and intended for people across all countries and in all time periods. It encompasses ancient history, starting from the creation of time, covers all time periods, and offers prophecies of the end time and eternity. The Bible is both one cohesive book and a library of 66 individual books. To become a skilled worker who "needeth not to be ashamed," we must learn to handle the Word of God with the same care and distinctions that God built into it.

Just as a skilled craftsman respects the nature of his materials—treating oak differently from pine, or granite differently from sandstone—a skilled Bible student must respect the various sections of God's Word. When studying the Bible, a foundational principle is that while all Scripture is ***for*** us, not all Scripture is written ***to*** us or ***about*** us.

Remembering that principle is key to unlocking the Bible's meaning. The Apostle Paul affirmed this principle:

> *"All Scripture is given by inspiration of God, and is profitable for doctrine, for reproof, for correction, for instruction in righteousness." (2 Timothy 3:16)*

Every word from Genesis to Revelation is meant for our learning and benefit. In the Bible's historical accounts, we can learn about God's holiness in the Levitical laws, His faithfulness in the promises made to Abraham, His love, mercy and grace given in His covenants, His justice in the judgments poured out on sinful nations, etc. However, this does not mean that every command or promise is directly addressed to us as members of the Church today. We must have a framework of rightly dividing to properly understand God's words.

Right division is an essential tool of biblical hermeneutics. You may be wondering what that means! Hermeneutics is the science and art of interpreting Scripture. It is a method of interpretation that enables us to distinguish between different people, covenants, time periods, and promises so we can apply God's Word correctly. This approach requires us to adhere to two non-negotiable rules that form the foundation of sound interpretation.

Rule #1: Context is King

More errors in biblical interpretation arise from ignoring context than from any other single mistake. A verse or passage, ripped from the words that surround it, can be made to mean almost anything—a practice often called "proof-texting." Proof-texting is defined as quoting isolated verses or passages while ignoring their original context.

A skilled workman never does this. He understands that to "cut straight," he must honor the setting in which the words were given. As one scholar wisely put it, "A text without a context is a pretext for a proof-text" (a pretext is a reason given in justification of a course of action). To avoid this, we must examine context at three crucial levels: historical, grammatical, and literary.

A. Historical Context: Who, What, To Whom & When?

The most direct way to rightly divide is to approach every passage with a set of investigative questions, much like a detective examining a piece of evidence. Considering the words, ask:

- **Who is speaking?** Is it God the Father, Jesus, a prophet, an apostle, a Pharisee, or someone else? The identity of the speaker is crucial for understanding the authority and intent behind the words. The words of Job's friends, for example, are recorded accurately in Scripture, but their counsel was flawed and later corrected by God Himself. Their words are not truths or principles for us to receive, despite the accuracy of the record of their words. **Qualifying the "who" is important.**

- **To whom is it spoken?** This is perhaps the most critical question. Is the message for the nation of Israel? The Church? Unbelieving Gentiles? A specific individual? Recognizing the intended audience is the first step in right division. The entire book of Deuteronomy, for example, is a series of addresses from Moses to the nation of Israel as they prepare to enter the Promised Land. It contains specific laws for their national life that do not apply directly to the Church. **Qualifying "to whom" is important.**

- **What is said and in what context?** In which dispensation, or period of God's administration, were the words given? Were they spoken before the Law, under the Law, during Jesus' earthly ministry, or after the establishment of the Church? God has interacted with humanity in different ways throughout history, and understanding these dispensations brings immense clarity. An example is the law to stone a woman caught in adultery (Deuteronomy 22:20-21). That law was given to ancient Israel under the Old Covenant and does not apply to the Church under the New Covenant. **Qualifying "what" and "when" is important.**

Although penned in the ancient Near East, the Bible's 66 books convey a message for the whole world—revealing who God is, His work, and His eternal plan for all creation. The message is timeless, universal, and profitable, but it must be understood in its proper historical framework to be rightly received.

B. Grammatical Context: Words & Sentences Matter

At its most basic level, "cutting straight" means paying close attention to the grammar—what is said, that is the words, sentences, and paragraphs as they were written.

- **Word Meanings:** A workman is careful with his words. We must seek to understand what the words meant to the original audience in their language at the time. Many Hebrew and Greek words have a richer meaning than their English translations. A simple word study can unlock profound meaning. For example, in John 21, Jesus asks Peter three times if he loves Him. The first two times, Jesus uses the Greek word agapaō (unconditional, divine love), while Peter responds with phileō (brotherly affection). The final time, Jesus switches to phileō, meeting Peter at his level. This nuance, lost in most English translations, is a powerful part of the exchange.

- **Surrounding Verses** (The Immediate Context): Individual verses must always be interpreted in light of the verses and paragraphs surrounding them. A classic example is the misuse of Philippians 4:13: "I can do all things through Christ who strengthens me." Without context, this verse is often treated as a blank check for personal ambition. However, the context of verses 11-12 reveals that Paul is specifically discussing his ability to be content in all circumstances, whether in poverty or in abundance. The power Christ gives him is for endurance through hardship, not for worldly achievement. Ignoring the surrounding sentences completely distorts the verse's true meaning. Another common error is in quoting Matthew 18:20 "For where two or three are gathered together in my name, there am I in the midst of them." The context of Matthew 18 is not about Jesus' presence (for He is always present, regardless of how many people are gathered). In context, the verse is about church discipline. Jesus is assuring that His authority is present even if only a small group of believers (two or three) undertake the difficult task of confronting sin.

C. Literary Context: Understanding the Genre

Again, the Bible is not a single book, but a library of books with various literary styles. Each must be read according to its own rules.

- **History/Narrative:** In the Old Testament, we have Joshua, Judges, Ruth, 1 and 2 Samuel, 1 and 2 Kings, 1 and 2 Chronicles, Ezra, Nehemiah, and Esther. These books record historical events. They tell us what happened, but not everything that happened is a model for us to follow. For example, the book of Judges describes a chaotic cycle of sin and apostasy. The book contains descriptive passages, not prescriptive commands for our behavior.

- **Law:** The books of Law include Genesis, Exodus, Leviticus, Numbers, and Deuteronomy. They contain God's commands to the nation of Israel under the Old Covenant. While they reveal God's holy character, we must rightly divide the Law to understand which commands were specific to Israel (i.e., dietary laws) and which reflect timeless moral principles (i.e., the moral law).

- **Poetry/Wisdom**: Job, Psalms, Proverbs, Ecclesiastes, and Song of Solomon (or Song of Songs) are the books of poetry and wisdom. They use vivid imagery, parallelism, and metaphor. We should not interpret them with the same strict literalism as historical narrative. For example, when the psalmist says God has "wings," it is a metaphor, meant to illustrate His protection. It's not a literal description.

- **Prophecy:** In the Old Testament, there are five books of the major prophets— Isaiah, Jeremiah, Lamentations, Ezekiel, and Daniel, and 12 books of the minor prophets—Hosea, Joel, Amos, Obadiah, Jonah, Micah, Nahum, Habakkuk, Zephaniah, Haggai, Zechariah, and Malachi. Prophecy often uses symbolic language to foretell of future events, however, it should be remembered that these symbols point to literal future realities. A dispensational approach insists that prophecies concerning Israel will be fulfilled by a literal, future nation of Israel, and they are not to be spiritualized and applied to the Church.

In the New Testament, there is one book of prophecy—Revelation—however, only chapters 1-3 are directly related to the Church. Chapters 4 and 5 give a glimpse into the Throne Room of Heaven, and with the beginning of chapter 6, the end times are unveiled with prophecies that relate to Israel and the nations only since the Church will have been taken to Heaven in the Rapture.

- **Epistles:** These are letters written to specific churches or people to address particular situations and teach doctrine. There are 21 epistles: Romans, 1 and 2 Corinthians, Galatians, Ephesians, Philippians, Colossians, 1 and 2 Thessalonians, 1 and 2 Timothy, Titus, Philemon, Hebrews, James, 1 and 2 Peter, 1, 2, and 3 John, and Jude. While the letters of Paul to the Churches present the primary source of doctrine for the Church, Paul's letters to others (Timothy, Titus, Philemon, and Hebrews) and the letters written by James, Peter, John, and Jude give clear instruction in righteousness for the Church.

- **Transitional Books:** The four Gospel accounts and the Book of Acts are both historical and transitional —each presenting accounts of the people, places, and lessons in first-century Israel during the lifetime of Jesus and immediately after. They also offer instruction in righteousness for the Church when rightly understood and rightly applied. Most of what is recorded in the Gospels was historical under the Old Covenant. It was only after the death, burial, resurrection, and ascension that the New Covenant replaced the Old Covenant. Furthermore, in the Book of Acts, we can clearly see a transition from the early Church's limited understanding of the gospel of saving grace to a fuller understanding of God's redemptive work. When God raised up Paul, He more fully revealed the riches of Christ to him and appointed him as the apostle to the Gentiles. It is through Paul's writings that we receive the clearest communications of God's purpose and plan for the Body of Christ (the Church).

Rule #2: Let Scripture Interpret Scripture

This is the golden rule of interpretation. Because the Bible is the inspired, inerrant Word of God, it is a perfectly consistent and coherent whole. It does not contradict itself. Therefore, the Bible is its own best commentary.

- **Harmonizing Passages:** A classic example is the apparent conflict between Paul and James on faith and works.

  Paul states in Romans 3:28 that we are *"justified by faith apart from the works of the law."*

  James 2:24 says *"a person is justified by what they do and not by faith alone."*

  Do those statements contradict? They seem to, but properly understood in context, they do not. A careful workman lays both passages side by side and harmonizes them. Paul is discussing our justification before God—our legal, positional standing, which is by faith alone. James, however, is discussing the evidence of that justification before men—our practical living, which should be walking in the Spirit. Real, saving faith is a living faith that inevitably produces good works. They are two sides of the same coin: one is our positional standing in Christ, the other is our practical living in the world but with the Holy Spirit as our guide. There is no contradiction when the statements are "rightly divided" into one being about justification and the other about sanctification.

- **Progressive Revelation:** We must also recognize that God revealed His plan progressively over time. He did not reveal everything to Adam, Abraham, or Moses. It can even be understood that God did not fully reveal His plan to the Body of Christ (the Church) until He raised up Paul. With progressive revelation recorded in the New Testament, we have a much greater understanding of God's purpose and plan. For example, the sacrificial system in Leviticus seems strange and bloody until we read the book of Hebrews, which explains that it was a temporary system of shadows, meant to point forward to the final, perfect sacrifice of Jesus Christ. The New Testament, therefore, is understood to fulfill and explain that which was presented in the Old Testament.

By diligently applying these two rules— 1) honoring context in all its forms and 2) letting Scripture interpret Scripture—we can move from being sometimes-confused readers to skilled workmen, confidently and accurately handling the Word of Truth.

Chapter 3

Essential Distinctions

Repeatedly, we stress that the Bible is far more than a random collection of ancient texts, stories, poetry, legal codes, and religious writings. It is a coherent, divinely inspired library of books that reveals God's plan as it unfolds over time. This unfolding or progressive revelation discloses God's eternal purposes, His redemptive plan for humanity, and His ultimate Kingdom.

From the patriarchs, such as Abraham, who received foundational promises, to the prophets, who received more detailed visions, and finally to the apostles, who were granted an even clearer understanding through the Holy Spirit, God's Word stands as a continuous narrative of redemption that illuminates the past and clearly points toward the future.

To navigate this grand story, the workman must learn to recognize the key signposts and divisions God Himself has placed within it. Failing to see these "cuts" is like trying to assemble a piece of furniture without distinguishing among screws, bolts, nails, panels, legs, supports, etc. The result is confusion and a structure that cannot stand. This chapter introduces some of the most critical distinctions that a Bible student must master to properly understand God's message in His Word.

The Divine Division of Scripture: Old & New Testaments

The most fundamental division every reader encounters is that of the Old and New Testaments. These two sections form the backbone of God's revelation to humanity. The great church father Augustine of Hippo (354-430 AD) wisely stated, "The New is in the Old concealed; the old is in the new revealed." This profound saying means that the Old Testament contains shadows, types, and prophecies that find their ultimate fulfillment and explanation in the New Testament. The sacrificial system, the priesthood, and the prophecies of a suffering servant make complete sense only in light of the Cross of Jesus Christ. Likewise, the New Testament constantly looks back to the Old Testament, revealing the profound significance of its events, laws, and characters in light of the person and work of Jesus Christ. Understanding this dynamic relationship is essential for rightly dividing the Word.

God's Different Administrations: Ages & Dispensations

A cornerstone of rightly dividing is understanding that throughout history, God has administered His purposes on earth in different ways. These distinct periods of administration are commonly referred to as dispensations. As already mentioned in our introduction, the Greek word "oikonomia" (translated dispensation) means "household management" or "stewardship." The word "dispensation" is found in 1 Corinthians 9:17, Ephesians 1:10, Ephesians 3:2, and Colossians 1:25, and it refers to God's dealing with humanity, in a particular way which has varied in different time periods.

It is crucial to think of a dispensation as a "stewardship." The New King James Bible even translates "oikonomia" as "stewardship" in two verses. A dispensation/stewardship is not the same as an "age." The next chapter will cover dispensations. Here, let's consider ages.

An "age" refers to a vast period of time, often marked by a major geological change to the earth or defined by a prominent feature of the time. Scripture speaks of three great ages:

- The Antediluvian Age: From Creation to the Flood.
- The Present Age: From the Flood to Christ's Second Coming.

- The Age of Ages: Encompassing the Millennial Kingdom and the Eternal State.

Within these ages, God has implemented different dispensations or stewardships for His interactions with His creation. Recognizing in which dispensation a passage belongs is critical for avoiding confusion about God's promises and commands.

The Kingdom of Heaven and the Kingdom of God

One of the most frequent sources of confusion comes from failing to distinguish between the "Kingdom of Heaven" and the "Kingdom of God." While the terms sometimes overlap, they refer to distinct concepts that must be rightly divided.

The Kingdom of Heaven is primarily a political and geographical term. It refers to the literal, physical abode and the reign of the King, the Messiah. During the time in which we live, known as the Church Age, the literal, physical Kingdom of Heaven is in Heaven--where Jesus is seated on the throne at the right hand of God the Father. However, God promised Israel that the Messiah would sit on the throne of David in Jerusalem, and reign over an earthly kingdom (Isaiah 9:6-7; Jeremiah 23:5-6; Luke 1:32-33). This Kingdom is yet to come. It is the Kingdom that John the Baptist and Jesus announced was "at hand" (near) for the nation of Israel (Matthew 3:2; 4:17) when Jesus, the promised Messiah, was on earth (near). When Israel's leaders rejected their Messiah/King, the establishment of this physical Kingdom on earth was postponed. It awaits its future fulfillment on earth when Christ returns in glory to rule the nations.

The Kingdom of God is a broader, more universal, and spiritual term. It refers to the realm of God's sovereign rule. In its present form, it is the spiritual reign of Christ in the hearts of believers. This Kingdom is not defined by physical territory but by "righteousness, and peace, and joy in the Holy Spirit" (Romans 14:17). Jesus reigns today as King in the lives of His followers, who have been "translated...into the Kingdom of [God's] dear Son"

(Colossians 1:13). Understanding this distinction prevents the error of trying to build a political, earthly kingdom now. That's a task reserved for Jesus Christ when He returns.

(Review the chart on the Kingdom of Heaven and the Kingdom of God found in the appendix.)

Christ's Threefold Office: Prophet, Priest, and King

Another essential distinction is recognizing the three messianic offices of Christ and their primary fulfillment in different dispensations.

- Christ as Prophet: In His earthly ministry, Jesus fulfilled the office of prophet. He was God's ultimate spokesman, speaking God's truth, calling Israel to repentance, and authenticating His message with miracles, signs, and wonders. Sadly, Israel, as a nation, rejected their Prophet-King (Luke 13:33-34).
- Christ as Priest: Currently, during this Church Age, Christ serves as our great High Priest. He is not on earth, but seated at the right hand of the Father in the holiest of Holy places and He ministers for us in the heavenly sanctuary (Hebrews 4:14; 8:1). He intercedes for believers, bringing our prayers to the Father, and mediating the New Covenant. He desires to intercede and mediate for all people, but sadly, many today reject the High Priest.
- Christ as King: While Jesus is now the King of the spiritual Kingdom of God and reigns in the hearts of all who are His, in the future, at His second coming, Jesus will take up His kingly office. He will return to earth not as a suffering servant, but as the "King of KINGS, and Lord of LORDS" (Revelation 19:16). He will establish His Millennial Kingdom (a 1,000 year earthly reign) and rule with righteousness and a rod of iron from God's holy city, Jerusalem.

Recognizing these distinct roles helps us to correctly interpret passages that speak of Christ's work and the nature of His Kingdom at different points on God's timeline.

The "Times"

Scripture also speaks about "eras"—although the Bible does not use that specific term. An era is a short time period and is referenced as "times" in these verses:

- The "times of ignorance" refers to the time period (era) before the full revelation of God in Christ, a time God "winked at" or overlooked in His great patience (Acts 17:30).
- The "times of the Gentiles" began with Babylon's conquest of Jerusalem and refers to the period during which Gentile powers dominated the Holy City (an era). Jesus stated this period would continue "until the times of the Gentiles be fulfilled" (Luke 21:24), making this also an age—a long period of time pointing to the completion of God's plan and a future restoration of Israel.
- The "times of refreshing" refers to the future period of national restoration and revitalization for Israel when their Messiah returns (Acts 3:19-21). This will be the time when Jesus returns with His Bride (the Church), establishes His earthly kingdom. He will then rule from Jerusalem in righteousness over all the earth, and Israel will be the lead nation.

Recognizing that we are living in the "times of the Gentiles" and in the dispensation of the Church clarifies that our mission is not one of political conquest but of spiritual ambassadorship. Our commission is to proclaim the gospel of grace. By grasping these essential distinctions, the workman can avoid the doctrinal confusion that arises from mixing precepts, promises, purposes, and plans intended for different people and different times. When one rightly divides the Word of Truth, one can appreciate the remarkable consistency of God's Word, His will, and His ways, and can rest confidently in the promises that truly belong to a child of God in the Church Age.

Chapter 4

A Biblical Timeline: Ages & Dispensations

Consider the Bible not as a flat, two-dimensional photograph, but as a three-dimensional, unfolding drama. History is moving from a starting point to a divine conclusion, and God has structured this story with clear divisions. Recognizing this framework is like having a map for the biblical world—without it, we can easily get lost.

Let's dive deeper into understanding ages and dispensations. We've already looked at them briefly, but now let's review and examine them more closely to understand the distinctions.

As we learned in the previous chapter, the broadest divisions in this timeline are ages, while the administrative periods within those ages are called dispensations. Grasping the distinction between these two concepts is crucial for a workman who desires to "cut straight."

The Three Great Ages

An Age, in biblical terms, represents a vast period of time, typically marked by a catastrophic physical change to the earth. Scripture reveals a divine timeline consisting of three such Ages.

- **The Antediluvian Age**—The World That Was: This age began at Creation and ended with the worldwide Flood of Noah's day. The Apostle Peter refers to this as "the world that then was" and describes its end as "being overflowed with water, perished" (2 Peter 3:6). It was a world vastly different from our own, characterized by a different environment and extreme human longevity. It began in perfection and ended in judgment.

- **The Present Age**—The Heavens and the Earth, Which Are Now: This is the age in which we currently live. It began with Noah and his family stepping out of the ark onto a cleansed earth, and it will conclude with the Second Coming of Jesus Christ. The Bible describes this age as a fallen and temporary world characterized by specific spiritual and moral conditions, standing in sharp contrast to "the age to come." Paul called it the "present evil age" (Galatians 1:4), a time when "the god of this age" (the devil) holds significant influence over the world's systems and seeks to blind the minds of unbelievers (2 Corinthians 4:4). Paul wrote that the "prince of the power of the air...works in the children of disobedience" (Ephesians 2:2) and that the wisdom of this age is earthly, unspiritual, and demonic, standing in opposition to God's wisdom (1 Corinthians 1:20).
- **The Age of Ages**—The World to Come: This future age begins with the physical return of Jesus Christ to the earth. It starts with His 1,000-year Millennial Kingdom in which Jesus will rule with righteousness over all the world, and after the 1,000 years the Eternal State begins. It will be the final and everlasting state of God's perfect kingdom, and the Bible describes it as "a new heaven and a new earth, wherein dwelleth righteousness" (2 Peter 3:13).

The Seven Dispensations (Stewardships)

While ages are vast chronological periods, remember that dispensations are the divine administrations, or stewardships, by which God governs humanity within those ages. The word "dispensation" (oikonomia) literally means "the law of the house" and refers to the order and regulations within a household. In each dispensation, God introduces a new test of man's obedience to a specific revelation of His will.

It is critical to note that the way of salvation has never changed. Salvation has always been by grace through faith. Some have taught that salvation in the Old Testament was by faith + works, citing the sacrificial system as a work. However, they fail to understand that the work of making sacrifice was simply a demonstration of faith by obedience. These same people also teach that salvation in the Tribulation will revert to faith + works, as in the Old Testament, but this can easily be biblically proven to be wrong. Salvation has always been, is now, and always will be by the grace of God given to those who come to Him in faith and trust.

What does change from one dispensation to another is the extent of the revelation given to mankind and the kind of response in faith desired by God. We should understand the Bible to be a book of progressive revelation, and each dispensation as God's testing of humanity in preparation for the fulfillment of His redemptive plan. Sadly, each dispensation ends in human failure, demonstrating mankind's absolute need for divine grace.

Differentiating the Dispensations (Stewardships)

A careful workman must understand the distinctions of the seven dispensations to avoid misapplying commands and promises. Every dispensation follows a tragic and repetitive pattern:

- Responsibility is given
- Rebellion follows
- Retribution (judgment) is executed
- God's sovereign grace provides a new way forward.

As we trace this pattern through history, it powerfully demonstrates humanity's consistent failure and God's unending love and unwavering faithfulness.

1. Dispensation of Innocence—*Antediluvian (Genesis 1:26-3:7)*

- Responsibility: This dispensation was man's state in the

Garden of Eden. Created in God's image, Adam and Eve were innocent, knowing neither good nor evil. They walked in perfect communion with their Creator in a perfect environment. Their test was one of simple obedience to a single, clear prohibition: "Of the tree of the knowledge of good and evil, thou shalt not eat of it: for in the day that thou eatest thereof thou shalt surely die" (Genesis 2:16-17). They were responsible for tending the garden and obeying this one command.

- Rebellion: Eve was deceived by the serpent's lie, "Ye shall not surely die," and Adam willfully joined her in disobedience, choosing his wife over his God. This act of rebellion plunged the human race into sin.

- Retribution: The judgment was immediate and sweeping. They were spiritually separated from God, their bodies began dying, their innocence was lost, shame entered their hearts, the earth was cursed, and they were expelled from the Garden. The curse of sin and death was pronounced upon them, upon the serpent, and upon the very ground itself (Genesis 3:14-19).

- Grace: Even in judgment, God's grace was present. Instead of condemning them forever, He promised a future Redeemer, the "seed of the woman," who would one day crush the serpent's head (Genesis 3:15). In a beautiful act of mercy, God Himself shed the first blood, making coats of skins to cover their nakedness—a foreshadowing of the substitutionary atonement of Christ.

2. Dispensation of Conscience—*Antediluvian (Genesis 3:8-8:22)*

- Responsibility: Driven from the Garden, humanity was now governed from within by conscience—an inward sense of right and wrong. The responsibility was to do good, restrain evil, and approach God through an acceptable blood sacrifice, the way of faith demonstrated by Abel (Genesis 4:4).

- Rebellion: This dispensation also ended in failure, as "the wickedness of man was great in the earth, and... every imagination of the thoughts of his heart was only evil continually" (Genesis 6:5). The period was also marked by a unique angelic intervention, as the "sons of God" (likely fallen angels) intermarried with human women, producing an unnatural offspring and further corrupting the human race (Genesis 6:1-4).

- Retribution: The judgment was the global Flood, a cataclysmic event that destroyed all land-dwelling, air-breathing life except for Noah and his family.

- Grace: God's grace was manifest in His warning to Noah, His detailed instructions for building the ark, and His preservation of a remnant of humanity and the animal kingdom to repopulate the earth.

3. **Dispensation of Human Government**—*Post-Diluvian (Genesis 8:16-11:32)*

- Responsibility: After the Flood, God established a new principle to restrain evil: human government. He gave humanity the authority to govern itself, instituting the solemn responsibility of capital punishment for murder to protect the sanctity of life: "Whoso sheddeth man's blood, by man shall his blood be shed: for in the image of God made he man," (Genesis 9:6).

- Rebellion: Despite this new beginning, human government quickly failed. Instead of scattering and filling the earth as commanded, humanity united in prideful rebellion at the Tower of Babel, seeking to make a name for themselves and build a civilization independent of God.

- Retribution: In judgment, God confused their languages, forcing them to scatter across the face of the earth, demonstrating that human unity apart from God leads only to confusion and division.

- Grace: In response to the failure of humanity as a whole, God's grace initiated a new program, narrowing His focus to one man and his family, through whom He would bring blessing to the entire world.

4. Dispensation of Preparation and Promise—*Patriarchal (Genesis 12:1-Exodus 19:25)*

- Responsibility: God called Abram out of paganism and made an unconditional covenant with him, promising him a land, a great nation of descendants, and a personal blessing that would extend to all families of the earth (Genesis 12:1-3). He also promised to bless those who would bless Abram and curse those who would curse him (Genesis 12:3). The covenant was passed down through the patriarchs: Abraham, Isaac, and Jacob. Their primary responsibility was simply to believe God's covenantal promises and walk by faith in the land He had given them.

- Rebellion: While the patriarchs are commended for their faith, this period was also marked by failure. They often wavered, doubted, and resorted to carnal means to fulfill God's promises. Ultimately, due to famine, Jacob's family left the promised land and settled in Egypt, where their descendants eventually fell into centuries of brutal slavery.

- Retribution: The judgment was 400 years of bondage in a foreign land—Egypt.

- Grace: God graciously heard the cries of His people, remembered His covenant with Abraham, and raised up Moses to deliver them from Egypt with a mighty hand. He was preparing to establish them as His own nation.

5. Dispensation of Law—*Legal (Exodus 19-Acts 2:4)*

- Responsibility: At Mount Sinai, God entered into a conditional covenant with the nation of Israel. He gave them the Mosaic Law, a detailed system of commandments and ordinances that governed their national, religious, and civil life. The Law was a "schoolmaster" intended to reveal God's perfect holiness and expose Israel's utter sinfulness, thereby leading them to see their need for a Savior (Galatians 3:24). Their responsibility was to keep God's holy Law.

- Rebellion: The history of Israel under the Law is a near-unbroken record of failure. From the golden calf at the foot of Sinai to the constant cycles of idolatry in the book of Judges and the rejection of the prophets, Israel proved incapable of keeping the Law. This dispensation reached its tragic climax when the nation officially rejected and crucified their promised Messiah, Jesus Christ.
- Retribution: The judgment for this ultimate act of rebellion was the destruction of Jerusalem in 70 A.D. and the worldwide dispersion of the Jewish people, which continues to this day.
- Grace: Even in Israel's failure to recognize their Messiah, God's grace abounded. The death of Christ, the greatest crime of humanity, became the very means of salvation for all who would believe.

6. Dispensation of the Church—*Ecclesiastical*
(Acts 2:4-Revelation 20:3)

- Responsibility: This is the present dispensation. It is a unique "parenthesis" in God's prophetic program for Israel. In this age, God is not dealing with a nation, but is calling out a new entity, the Church, the Body of Christ, composed of individuals, both Jews and Gentiles, who are saved by grace through faith alone. Our responsibility is to be guided by the moral law, walking by the power of the indwelling Holy Spirit, loving one another, and fulfilling the Great Commission by sharing the gospel of saving and sanctifying grace with all people.
- Rebellion: Scripture prophecies that this dispensation will

not end well. Rather than a worldwide revival, there will be widespread apostasy and rejection of sound doctrine (1 Timothy 4:1; 2 Timothy 3:1-5). The world system will become increasingly hostile to the truth of who Christ is, His works, and His Word.

- Retribution: This dispensation will not end in judgment for the believer, but in deliverance. It will culminate with the Rapture of the Church, when Christ will bodily resurrect all Church Age believers—those died with faith in Him and those who remain alive. He will take them to be with Him in Heaven, prior to the final period of God's judgment, the Tribulation, the seven years in which God's wrath will be poured out in judgment of the world's sin.
- Grace: This entire dispensation is the ultimate expression of God's grace, an unmerited favor extended to all who believe in the finished work of Christ. Its key distinctions include the permanent indwelling of the Holy Spirit, the believer's absolute security in Christ, our position as heavenly citizens, and our guaranteed promise of a home in Heaven with our Savior.

The Tribulation — *After The Rapture of the Church, the Seventieth Week of Daniel begins (Daniel 9:24-27).* This will be a seven year period. The Bible describes it as the time of Jacob's trouble (Jeremiah 30:7), a time of trouble (Daniel 12:1, 11) and tribulation (Deuteronomy 4:30, Mark 13:25). Jesus and John spoke of the Great Tribulation (Matthew 24:21 ff., Revelation 7:14). During this time, God will call to Himself a believing remnant from the nation of Israel (Isaiah 10:20-22, Zechariah 13:8-9, Micah 2:12). They will come to know Jesus as their promised Messiah, and they will repent and be preserved through the judgments of God. We commonly call this time The Tribulation. Historically, the Tribulation has not been considered a dispensation, but rather a parenthesis between the Church Age and the Messianic Age.

7. Dispensation of the Messianic Kingdom— the *Millennial Reign of Christ on Earth (Revelation 20:4-6)*

- Responsibility: After the judgment of the Tribulation, Christ will return to earth with His saints to establish His long-promised kingdom. Satan will be bound, and Christ will rule from Jerusalem with absolute righteousness and justice. The curse on creation will be partially lifted, and the earth will be restored to Eden-like conditions. The responsibility of humanity during this time will be direct and willing obedience to the visible, reigning King.

- Rebellion: Incredibly, even under these perfect conditions, this dispensation will end in failure. Satan will be loosed for a short time at the end of the 1,000 years, and he will find a vast multitude of people born during the Millennium who will choose to join him in a final, futile rebellion against Christ (Revelation 20:7-9). This proves definitively that the problem of humanity is not culture or environment. The problem is the unrepentant heart.

- Retribution: The judgment will be swift and final. God will send fire down from Heaven that will devour the rebels. This will be followed by the bodily resurrection of the dead who died without faith. They will stand before God at the Great White Throne Judgment, be judged for their works, and be found wanting.

- Grace: Following this final judgment, God will renew the heavens and the earth by fire, purging all corruption in preparation for the Eternal State.

*** The New Heaven and New Earth***

Ephesians 1:10 calls this "the dispensation of the fullness of times" when God will "gather together in one all things in Christ." We call it eternity!

This is God's New Beginning, His restoration of the shalom and perfection of the Garden. There will no longer be any test, any failure, or any judgment, for there will be no sin and no sinners. Sin has been eternally put away, and God will be "all in all" (1 Corinthians 15:28) for all eternity.

> *He that sat upon the throne said, Behold, I make all things new. And he said unto me, Write: for these words are true and faithful. (Revelation 21:5)*

Chapter 5

Unveiling the Mystery of the Church

Of the many profound truths unlocked by rightly dividing the Word, it is critical that we understand the unique nature of the Church. A failure to see the Church for what it is—a completely new creation, distinct from Israel—is the source of endless theological confusion. Many errors arise, including:

- Replacement/supersessionist theology—the church permanently replaces Israel, canceling Israel's specific future promises.
- Kingdom-now theology—treats the present church age as the full messianic kingdom, producing over-realized triumphalism.
- Covenant-flattening—collapses Abrahamic, Davidic, and New Covenants into a generic "church covenant," obscuring Israel's national role.
- Prophetic allegorizing—spiritualizes Israel/Zion/Jerusalem texts so "Israel" is read as "church" in prophecy.
- Misapplied national mandates—imports Israel's theocratic, territorial, and political calling into the church's present mission.
- Eschatological compression—blurs or denies Israel's future repentance, restoration, and kingdom role by folding all stages into a single, mostly spiritual end.

The Church is not simply a "New Testament version" of the nation of Israel. It is not Israel 2.0. The Church, which the Bible calls the Body and the Bride of the Lord Jesus Christ, is an entirely new living organism. It is a spiritual entity that had no existence prior to Jesus' resurrection and glorification, and has no parallel in the Old Testament times. Its origin, composition, mission, and destiny are all entirely distinct from that of national Israel. The Apostle Paul, to whom this truth was fully revealed, calls the church a "mystery" that was "hidden in God" for ages and is only now being made known. (Ephesians 3:9)

The Mountain Peaks of Prophecy

To understand this mystery, imagine the Old Testament prophets as men standing on a mountain ridge, looking out across the landscape of God's prophetic plan. From their vantage point, they could see the mountain peaks in the distance.

While the first two mountain peaks were prophesied, they were not clearly seen. The prophets' gaze was focused on the Kingdom Age, the third mountain peak that was Israel's hope and almost complete obscured their vision of the fourth peak, the Perfect Age/Eternity.

- **The First Peak**: They saw the mountain of Messiah's suffering, and prophesied in stunning detail of a coming King who would be born of a virgin, would be rejected by His own people, and would suffer, bleed, and die for the sins of the world (Isaiah 7:14; Isaiah 53).

- **The Second Peak:** The prophets saw only a prophetic glimpse of the smaller second peak (The Tribulation).

- **The Third Peak**: Further in the distance, the prophets clearly saw the mountain of Messiah's glory. They prophesied of the day when the King born in Bethlehem, but rejected by His people, would vanquish His enemies, deliver Israel, and establish an everlasting kingdom of peace and righteousness on the earth, reigning from Jerusalem (Zechariah 14; Isaiah 9:6-7).

- **The Fourth Peak**: Obscured in their vision, yet whispered of in prophecy, is the fourth, most glorious mountain -- Eternity, the Perfect Age.

- **The Valley**: The prophets were unable to see the long, deep, and wide valley that lay between the first and second mountain peaks. From their perspective, the suffering and the glory appeared to be part of one continuous event. They could not perceive the vast expanse of time that would separate Christ's first coming from His second coming, nor did they understand there would be two comings of one Messiah.

A Parenthesis—The Church

Hidden in the valley is the Church Age, a divine parenthesis in God's prophetic timeline for the nation of Israel. When Israel rejected their Messiah, God temporarily set the nation aside—though not forever (Romans 11:25-26), because He that promised is faithful (Hebrews 10:23). The Church Age is not prophesied of, but only whispered of, in the Old Testament. It is the dispensation in which a heavenly people are called out from among both Jews and Gentiles to be one body in Christ.

The Apostle Paul was given the unique ministry of revealing this "mystery of Christ," which he explains was "in other ages not made known unto the sons of men, as it is now revealed unto his holy apostles and prophets by the Spirit; That the Gentiles should be fellow heirs, and of the same body, and partakers of his promise in Christ by the gospel" (Ephesians 3:4-6). This "one new man" (Ephesians 2:15) is something entirely different from anything that came before.

Critical Distinctions Between Israel & the Church

To be a workman who cuts straight, one must learn to draw sharp lines of distinction between Israel and the Church. Confusing their identities, promises, and destinies leads to a tangle of misinterpretation. Understanding these distinctions is profoundly liberating. It means that Christians today are not under the laws given to Israel. We are not required to keep the ceremonial and civil laws of the Jews; and the moral law (The Ten Commandments) is for our instruction in righteousness. It cannot condemn us, because Jesus fulfilled the Law for us and we live in liberty (Galatians 5:1) and rest (Matthew 11:29). Our relationship with God is not based on national identity but on the grace of God given to us through personal faith in the finished work of Jesus Christ.

Our Heavenly Calling and Commission

Recognizing the Church as this mysterious parenthesis in God's prophetic timeline for the nation of Israel allows us to embrace our unique identity, calling, and hope in this present age. As the Body of Christ, we are not looking for, or trying to build, an earthly kingdom now—that task is reserved for the King of kings when He returns. Our citizenship is in heaven, and from that position, we function as ambassadors for Christ (2 Corinthians 5:20). Our commission is not political, but spiritual. We are called to proclaim the "gospel of the grace of God" (Acts 20:24), inviting everyone to find reconciliation with Him through Jesus Christ.

This understanding clarifies our mission and focuses our energy. We are not called to reform the world's political systems, but to rescue people out of the world through the power of the gospel. This glorious task will continue until the "fullness of the Gentiles be come in" (Romans 11:25), at which point our Blessed Hope (Titus 2:13) will be realized. Christ will descend from Heaven with a shout, the dead in Christ will rise first, and we who are alive and remain will be caught up together with them to meet the Lord in the air (1 Thessalonians 4:16-17). That's the Rapture! And at that moment, the dispensation of the Church Age will close, and God will turn His full attention back to His prophetic program for the nation of Israel, beginning the final seven years of judgment we call The Tribulation. At the end of the seven years, Jesus will return and establish His earthly kingdom.

Critical Distinctions Between The Kingdom of God and The Kingdom of Heaven

Having already addressed the two Kingdoms, it's important to reiterate it here, note the distinctions, and the biblical references.

God's original intent in the Garden of Eden was a united kingdom on earth, both spiritual and physical, inhabited by those created in His image. Adam and Eve were sinless, but sin entered the world when they disobeyed God's only command. It is said that they died spiritually, but also note that the perfect spiritual kingdom ceased to exist. By their sin, they broke their relationship with God, and He banished them from the Garden. Yet, in His mercy, God promised that one day He would send a Rescuer who would restore all things. First, the Rescuer would make a way for man to be restored to union with his Creator in the spiritual Kingdom of God; and in His perfect time, He would bring peace and righteousness in a future physical Kingdom of Heaven on earth.

The Kingdom of God in the Church Age

Having been forgiven of sins and born again, believers enter the Kingdom of God, spiritually. The Holy Spirit is the "mark" of every citizen in this kingdom and the guarantee of salvation, eternal life, and all future promises, including the future Kingdom of Heaven on earth.

The Kingdom of God is an unseen, spiritual kingdom.

> *Romans 14:17 For the kingdom of God is not meat and drink; but righteousness, and peace, and joy in the Holy Ghost.*

The Kingdom of God is present here on earth for every believer.

> *Luke 17:20–21 ...The kingdom of God comes not with observation: Neither shall they say, Lo here! or, lo there! for, behold, the kingdom of God is within you.*

As citizens of this kingdom, our King rules over our hearts and minds.

The Kingdom of Heaven

The Kingdom of Heaven is the place where God dwells. It is a literal, physical kingdom. During Jesus' earthly ministry, this kingdom was declared to be near, because Jesus was dwelling with man and preparing the Jews to recognize their King. Jesus preached, "The Kingdom of Heaven is at hand [near]" (Matthew 4:17), and He instructed His disciples to do the same (Matthew 10:7).

During the current Church Age, the Kingdom of Heaven remains where King Jesus dwells—sitting on His throne, at the right hand of the Father, in the Heaven of heavens, or the Third Heaven as the Bible calls it. All born-again believers are citizens of the Kingdom of Heaven and will go there at death or The Rapture.

One day, Jesus will return and fulfill God's plan of restoring the earth and bringing shaloam (peace) to the people. He will:

- Establish His Kingdom on earth.
- Rule in righteousness from a new temple in Jerusalem.
- Reign with His Bride, the Church, at His side.

It's important to understand that the Church, the Bride of Christ, will rule with Christ in this restored kingdom (Revelation 5:10, 20:4-6; 1 Corinthians 6:2-3; 2 Timothy 2:12); and Israel will be the lead nation having received fulfillment of God's promises to Abraham to be a blessing and a light to the nations (Genesis 18:18, Isaiah 49:6).

Citizenship in the Kingdoms

The present age is spiritually glorious, the coming kingdom will be both spiritually and physically glorious, and the Eternal State that follows will be magnificent, exceeding what we can imagine and with glory and joy beyond our comprehension.

Paul's prayer for the Ephesians beautifully summarizes this dual reality. In his prayer, Paul connects our identity as citizens of the Kingdom of Heaven ("the whole family in heaven and earth") with the reality of Christ dwelling in us while we remain on earth in the spiritual Kingdom of God ("the riches of His glory, to be strengthened with might through His Spirit in the inner man").

> *For this reason I bow my knees to the Father of our Lord Jesus Christ, from whom the whole family in heaven and earth is named, that He would grant you, according to the riches of His glory, to be strengthened with might through His Spirit in the inner man, that Christ may dwell in your hearts through faith; that you, being rooted and grounded in love, may be able to comprehend with all the saints what is the width and length and depth and height; to know the love of Christ which passes knowledge; that you may be filled with all the fullness of God. (Ephesians 3:14–19)*

<*}}}><

Chapter 6

The Great Divide—From Old Covenant Law to New Covenant Grace

Of all the distinctions necessary for "rightly dividing the word of truth," none is more foundational or more liberating than understanding the difference between the Old Covenant and the New Covenant. This is not merely a change in rules; it is a complete and total shift in the very basis of God's relationship with humanity.

The failure to make this rightly divided "cut" will lead to wrongly understanding Scripture. Grasping this division is the key to walking in the freedom, assurance, and joy that Christ secured for every believer. Mixing the Old Covenant and the New Covenant is like mixing concrete with water from a salt marsh; the resulting structure will inevitably crumble.

As we examine the two covenants, let's remember first their similarity. Both covenants offered salvation by grace through faith in God as He was revealed. This is biblically supported by Hebrews chapter 11 in which is found a record of the faith-fueled works of Old Testament saints that concludes with:

> *These all died in faith, not having received the promises, but having seen them afar off were assured of them, embraced them... (Hebrews 11:13)*

The Old Covenant: A System of Grace under Law

After delivering the nation of Israel from 400 years of slavery in Egypt, God gathered them at the foot of Mount Sinai and established a national covenant with them. This covenant, often called the Mosaic Law or simply "the Law," was a detailed, holy system of commandments, statutes, and ordinances that governed every aspect of Israel's life—everything from their worship and civil conduct to their diet and hygiene. It is crucial to understand that God made this covenant exclusively with the nation of Israel. It was not given to the Gentiles, nor was it ever intended to be the rule of life for the Church.

The Mosaic Covenant was a unique, conditional agreement God made with His chosen people:

> *"If ye will obey my voice indeed, and keep my covenant, then ye shall be a peculiar treasure unto me above all people." (Exodus 19:5)*

The purpose of the Law was twofold, and neither purpose was to provide a means of salvation.

1. Given to Reveal God's Holiness: The intricate demands of the Law, including its moral, civil, and ceremonial aspects, demonstrated the perfect righteousness and absolute holiness of God. It set a standard as perfect as God Himself, showing Israel the kind of character required to stand in His presence.

2. Given to Reveal Man's Sinfulness: Because no fallen human could ever perfectly keep its commands, the Law served as a divine mirror. Its purpose was not to make men righteous, but to reveal man's unrighteousness. As the Apostle Paul explains, "by the deeds of the law there shall no flesh be justified in his sight: for by the law is the knowledge of sin" (Romans 3:20). The Law was designed to silence every mouth and prove the whole world guilty before God (Romans 3:19).

Paul vividly describes the Law's function in his letter to the Galatians, calling it our "schoolmaster [tutor] to bring us unto Christ, that we might be justified by faith" (Galatians 3:24). Like a strict guardian for a child, the Law's purpose was to restrain, guide, and protect Israel until the way of faith in Christ was fully revealed. It was a temporary system designed to expose their sin, prove their helplessness, and create a desperate need for a Savior who could fulfill its demands on their behalf.

The New Covenant: A System of Grace in Liberty

The New Covenant is not an updated or modified version of the Old. It is an entirely new agreement, established on "better promises" (Hebrews 8:6). Its foundation is not based on the works of man but on the finished work of Jesus Christ. At the Last Supper, Jesus took the cup and declared, "This cup is the new testament [covenant] in my blood, which is shed for you" (Luke 22:20).

Under this new system, the governing principle is freedom by grace. This is the revolutionary truth that Paul declares with thunderous force in Romans 6:14: "For sin shall not have dominion over you: for you are not under the law, but under grace". For believers today—members of the Church, the Body of Christ—the Old Covenant Law is not our rule of life. We are dead to the Law through the body of Christ (Romans 7:4), and we have been freely given the perfect righteousness of Christ the moment we believed (2 Corinthians 5:21). This is not a reward for our efforts but an unmerited gift received by grace through faith alone (Ephesians 2:8-9).

Jesus did not simply set the Law aside; He fulfilled it completely (Matthew 5:17). His sinless life met every one of its righteous demands, and His sacrificial death on the cross paid its penalty for sin in full. Because Christ is the "end of the law for righteousness to every one that believes" (Romans 10:4), the believer is forever free from the Law's condemnation and its entire system of works-based righteousness.

Practical Consequences for the Believer

Understanding this monumental shift from Grace under Law to Grace in Liberty clears up countless passages that confuse those who do not rightly divide the Word. Believers are no longer bound by the specific regulations given to national Israel under the Mosaic Covenant. To attempt to place oneself back under any part of that system is to "fall from grace" (Galatians 5:4)—not to lose one's salvation, but to fall from the high principle of grace back down to the low principle of human effort.

Consider these practical examples of liberation from the Law:

- Dietary Laws: The book of Leviticus outlines a complex set of laws distinguishing between "clean" and "unclean" foods for Israel. These laws served a ceremonial purpose to mark Israel as a people set apart. Under the New Covenant, this system is obsolete. Jesus Himself "declared all foods clean" (Mark 7:19), and the Holy Spirit confirmed this to Peter in a vision, stating, "What God has cleansed you must not call common." (Acts 10:15). Christians are free to eat whatever they choose, and it should be always with thanksgiving to God.

- Sabbath Observance: The keeping of the seventh-day Sabbath was a specific sign of the Mosaic Covenant between God and the nation of Israel (Exodus 31:16-17). For the Church, the rigid legal requirement of Sabbath-keeping has been fulfilled in Christ. He Himself is our Sabbath rest (Hebrews 4:9-10). The early church met on Sunday, the first day of the week, to celebrate the resurrection, but there is no command in the New Testament epistles for believers to observe any specific day. Paul makes it clear that this is a matter of personal conscience, not a divine command: "One man esteemeth one day above another: another esteemeth every day alike. Let every man be fully persuaded in his own mind" (Romans 14:5). To bind Christians to Sabbath-keeping is to place them back under a yoke of bondage from which Christ has set them free.

- The Tithe: Tithing, the practice of giving ten percent of one's increase, was a requirement under the Mosaic Law to support the Levitical priesthood and the national worship system of Israel. In the New Covenant, the principle of giving is transformed. The standard is not a legalistic ten percent, but rather a generous, cheerful, and proportional giving. Paul instructs the Corinthians, "Every man according as he purposeth in his heart, so let him give; not grudgingly, or of necessity: for God loveth a cheerful giver" (2 Corinthians 9:7). The motivation is not law, but love.

- The Temple System: Under the Old Covenant, the Tabernacle and later the Temple in Jerusalem were the designated places where God's presence dwelt and where priests offered sacrifices for sin. This entire system was a shadow pointing to the reality that is Christ (Hebrews 10:1). Today, there is no physical "house of God" or earthly priesthood for the believer. Christ is our great High Priest (Hebrews 4:14), His one-time sacrifice is sufficient for all sin for all time (Hebrews 10:12), and the body of every believer is now the temple of the Holy Spirit (1 Corinthians 6:19).

Living under the New Covenant grace does not mean living without a standard. And while we might say we are not under the Law, the moral law still remains as good and profitable for our lives (Romans 7:12). As Christians, we have a new motivation and a new source of power. Instead of being motivated by the fear of punishment under the external commands of the Law, we are motivated by love for the One who redeemed us. We are empowered to live righteously not by our own strength, but by the indwelling Holy Spirit who produces His fruit in us (Galatians 5:22-23). This is the heart of the New Covenant and the glorious freedom of the Christian life. Remember this:

The Law commands from a distance.
The Spirit transforms from within.

<*}}}><

Chapter 7

Who Is The Audience?
Who is the Author?

Now that we have established the foundational principles and the grand timeline of God's redemptive plan, let's move to the practical application of rightly dividing. This section will serve as a hands-on guide, reinforcing the core principles of rightly dividing. We'll start with simple, investigative questions: Who? What? When? Where? and Why? This method, rooted in careful observation of the text, transforms Bible study from a confusing or intimidating exercise into a rewarding discovery of God's truth. By consistently asking these questions, the student of the Word can "cut straight" and accurately handle the precious truths God has revealed.

Who is the Audience?

The Apostle Paul provides the divine categories for us in 1 Corinthians 10:32: "Give none offense, neither to the Jews, nor to the Gentiles [Greeks], nor to the church of God." Scripture, therefore, identifies two kinds of people, Jews and Gentiles, and one specific body of people, the Church. A failure to distinguish the intended audience for any given passage of Scripture is the number one cause of doctrinal confusion. It leads to misapplying promises and commands, which can create spiritual anxiety, false hope, and/or unbiblical practices. While all Scripture is for us and is profitable for our learning, not all Scripture is written to us or about us. To determine the audience, a workman must ask two related questions.

Who is the Author?

First, identify the human author God used to pen the words. Is the author an Old Testament prophet like Isaiah, speaking primarily to the nation of Israel about their sin and future restoration? Is it a King of Israel, like Solomon in Ecclesiastes who wrote from a perspective of life "under the sun" apart from divine revelation? Or David in the Psalms? In the New Testament, is it the Apostle Paul, writing a letter to a specific local church? Or Peter, James, John, or Jude writing about how to live in Christ? The author's identity, his historical setting, and his specific ministry are foundational to understanding the message he's been given by God.

Who is the Original Audience?

Second, identify the people to whom the words were originally written or spoken.

- Were the words addressed to the nation of Israel under the Old Covenant?
- Were they addressed to the Church, the Body of Christ, under the New Covenant?
- Were they addressed to unbelieving Gentiles?
- Or were they spoken to a specific individual, like Timothy or Philemon, and for a particular purpose?

Note: Most of the verses in this book are from the King James Bible, and there's a good reason why. In the KJV, we can distinguish between singular and plural pronouns (thee, thou, etc./ye, you, etc.). This makes the KJV a good reference Bible if you don't use it regularly. Understand these distinctions:

- If the pronoun starts with a "t," it is singular: thou, thee, thy, thine.
- If it begins with a "y," consider it plural: ye, you, your, yours.

Read carefully, and you will see that many promises are made to the individual rather than to a group corporately. Watch carefully for those promises that are given to thee in a very personal way.

Now, let's consider several key sections of Scripture to see how understanding the audience brings immediate clarity.

Key Example: The Book of Leviticus

The Book of Leviticus contains a highly detailed system of laws, sacrifices, and regulations for purity and worship. When one does not rightly divide, this book can be baffling and seem utterly irrelevant. But when we ask, "Who is the audience?" the answer becomes clear. Leviticus 1:1-2 states, "And the Lord called unto Moses, and spake unto him out of the tabernacle of the congregation, saying, Speak unto *the children of Israel*, and say unto them..." The audience is unequivocally the nation of Israel under the Old Covenant.

These laws about animal sacrifices, dietary restrictions (clean and unclean foods), and the Levitical priesthood were given specifically to Israel. While we, as members of the Church, can learn profound truths about God's holiness, the seriousness of sin, and the necessity of a substitutionary sacrifice, these specific regulations are not commands for us today. We are not under this system. To take laws from Leviticus and try to apply them to a Christian's life today is a fundamental error in rightly dividing.

Key Example: The Olivet Discourse (Matthew 24-25)

In Matthew 24, Jesus' disciples ask Him, "what shall be the sign of thy coming, and of the end of the world [translated "age" in some Bibles]?" (Matthew 24:3). Jesus' response, known as the Olivet Discourse, is a detailed prophetic sermon about the events leading up to His Second Coming. Unfortunately, many Christians read this passage and become confused or fearful, applying its warnings directly to themselves.

However, when we ask, "Who is the audience?" we see that Jesus is speaking directly to His Jewish disciples under the Old Covenant, and answering a question about the end of the age from a Jewish perspective. The content of the sermon confirms this:

- Jesus speaks of the Jews fleeing from Judea (v. 16).
- Jesus warns them to pray that their flight is not on the Sabbath day (v. 20), which is a uniquely Jewish observance.
- Jesus describes a period of "great tribulation, such as was not since the beginning of the world" (v. 21)—the time which the prophet Daniel identified as the 70th week of God's prophetic plan for Israel (Daniel 9:24-27).

This passage is primarily for and about the Jewish people who will live through the future Tribulation period after the Church has been raptured and take to Heaven. While we can learn about God's sovereignty and the certainty of His coming judgment, His specific commands and warnings in this passage are not for the Church. The Church's hope is not to endure the Tribulation, but to be delivered from it by Jesus in the Rapture (1 Thessalonians 1:10; 5:9).

Key Example: The Book of Ephesians

In stark contrast, the Epistle to the Ephesians is written directly to the Church. Paul addresses his letter "to the saints which are at Ephesus, and to the faithful in Christ Jesus" (Ephesians 1:1). The content of this book is a deep dive into the "mystery" of the Church, the Body of Christ.

- It lays out the believer's heavenly position "in Christ" (Chapter 1-3).
- It details our spiritual blessings in heavenly places (1:3).
- It explains that Jew and Gentile are made "one new man" in Christ (2:15).

- It then provides practical instructions for Christian living under the New Covenant (Chapters 4-6).

Ephesians was written both *for us* and directly *to us* as members of the Church. The promises, commands, and doctrines in this epistle are ours to claim.

Distinguishing "To Me" vs. "For Me"

This distinction between what is written *to me* versus what is written *for me*, for my learning, is the essence of the first step in rightly dividing. For example, we can learn about God's character from His promise to Israel to give them the land of Canaan—but that specific promise is *not to* the Church. We are a heavenly people with a heavenly inheritance (Ephesians 1:3,11,13-14; 1 Peter 1:3–4). We can be encouraged by Jesus' command to His disciples to "sell what you have, and give alms" (Luke 12:33) as they awaited the imminent kingdom—but that command is *not for* believers in the Church Age. We are to give freely, thoughtfully, and cheerfully, in proportion to how God has prospered us, rather than by a fixed percentage as commanded in Israel's tithe (1 Corinthians 16:2; 2 Corinthians 9:6–8).

By consistently asking, "Who is the audience?" the workman learns to "cut straight," leaving promises for Israel with Israel and taking promises for the Church for himself. This simple question dissolves countless apparent contradictions and allows the beautiful, consistent tapestry of God's Word to come into clear view.

Chapter 8

What, When, and Where? Digging into the Context

After identifying the audience of a passage, the skilled workman's next step is to dig deeper into the context of what was said. This involves a grammatical approach—asking what the words actually mean—and a historical approach—considering the time, culture, and setting in which they were written. To do this effectively, three more crucial questions must be asked:

1. What was spoken?
2. When was it spoken?
3. Where was it spoken?

Answering these questions protects us from misinterpreting a text by forcing us to honor its specific circumstances. It keeps us from "spiritualizing" away the plain meanings or misapplying commands that were tied to a specific time and place.

What Was Spoken? Discerning Principle, Precept, or Promise

First, we must carefully analyze what is being communicated. Is the passage a timeless principle, a temporary precept, or a specific promise? Making this distinction is vital for correct application.

- **Principles** are timeless, universal truths about the character and nature of God and His will for humanity. For example, "the wages of sin is death" (Romans 6:23) is a principle that is true in every dispensation. The principle that "without faith it is impossible to please Him" (Hebrews 11:6) applied to Adam, Abraham, David, et.al., as well as to believers today. **God's principles are foundational truths. They transcend dispensational boundaries.**

- **Precepts** are specific commands or rules given to a particular group of people for a particular time. The command given to Israel that they were not to eat pork (Leviticus 11:7) was a precept for them under the Mosaic Law. It is not a command for the Church. The command for the disciples to "go not into the way of the Gentiles" during Jesus' early ministry (Matthew 10:5) was a temporary precept for that specific mission. It was later superseded by the Great Commission to make disciples of all nations (Matthew 28:19). **A workman must be careful not to elevate a temporary precept to the level of a timeless principle.**

- **Promises** are specific commitments of God made to specific people. God promised Abraham a literal piece of land—the land of Canaan (Genesis 15:18). This is a specific, eternal, and unconditional promise to Israel. While we can learn from this about God's faithfulness (a principle), the promise of that specific land is not a promise to the Church. Our promised "land" is spiritual and heavenly (1 Peter 1:4). **Not considering to whom God's promises were made leads to significant errors, particularly in eschatology.**

When Was It Spoken? The Importance of the Dispensational Setting

As we have seen, God has administered His plan through different dispensations, or stewardships, throughout history. A command given in one dispensation may be entirely out of place in another. To rightly divide, we must always ask, "When was this written?"

The four Gospels (Matthew, Mark, Luke, and John) provide a key example of why this is so important. These books are records of a crucial transitional period. While they are in the New Testament section of our Bibles, the events they record take place almost entirely under the Dispensation of Law. Jesus was born "under the law" (Galatians 4:4), and He ministered to the "lost sheep of the house of Israel" (Matthew 15:24) under that system. The Church did not yet exist.

Therefore, we must be cautious when applying Jesus' commands in the Gospels directly to the Church. For example, in the Sermon on the Mount, Jesus upholds the standard of the Law, even intensifying it (Matthew 5:17-48). He is demonstrating the true, perfect righteousness required to enter the Kingdom of Heaven (vs. 48). This was given to a Jewish audience under the Old Covenant to reveal their desperate need of a righteousness they could not attain.

Jesus was not laying down "rules of life" for the Church. The Church's rules of life are found most explicitly in the Pauline epistles, which were written after the cross and the birth of the Church to explain both our positional standing and our practical living in Christ.

Consider another example: The "Great Commission." Matthew 28:19-20 is a commission given by the resurrected Christ to believers in the Church Age. However, an earlier commission in Matthew 10, in which Jesus tells His disciples to go only to Israel and proclaim that the "kingdom of heaven is at hand," was specific to that time in His earthly ministry. Rightly dividing the "when" keeps us from mixing these two commissions.

Where Was It Spoken? Understanding the Geographical and Cultural Setting

Finally, understanding a passage's geographical and cultural setting can provide valuable insight. The Bible was written in a specific part of the world with its own customs, idioms, and agricultural cycles. While its message is universal, its context is often local.

For example, when Jesus speaks of a shepherd who leaves the ninety-nine sheep to find the one that is lost (Luke 15), He uses an illustration that His agrarian audience would have immediately understood. They would have deeply felt the value of every single sheep, the dangers of the wilderness, and the joy of the shepherd. Understanding this adds richness and depth to understand "the what."

Similarly, Paul wrote his letters to specific audiences—real churches in real cities like Corinth, Ephesus, and Philippi, each with its own unique cultural problems. His letter to the Corinthians addresses issues of rampant immorality, divisions, and spiritual pride that were characteristic of that bustling, pagan seaport. Knowing something about the city of Corinth helps us understand why Paul had to address these specific issues so forcefully. His instructions were not abstract theological treatises; they were urgent pastoral responses to real-life situations.

By consistently applying this three-part evaluation of What? When? and Where? the student of the Word can "cut straight" and accurately handle the precious truths God has revealed. This careful observation of the text prevents us from lifting verses out of their God-given context, and allows us to see the Bible for what it is: a progressive, coherent, and perfectly crafted revelation of God's unchanging character and His unfolding plan for the ages.

Chapter 9

Why Does It Matter?

The Transformative Power of Right Division

Having laid out the essential questions of practical application, we arrive at the most important question of all: Why? Why go to all this trouble? Why is it so critical to learn to distinguish between Jew, Gentile, and the Church? Why memorize dispensations or differentiate between covenants? Does "rightly dividing" really matter for the average Christian's daily life and walk with God? The answer is an emphatic "yes!"

Rightly dividing the Word of Truth is not an abstract academic exercise for theologians. It is a transformative discipline that has profound and practical consequences for every believer. It is the difference between a faith that is sometimes confused, anxious, and unstable, and a faith that is clear, confident, and firmly grounded in the truth of God's Word. Learning to "cut straight" resolves apparent contradictions, clarifies our unique identity in Christ, and liberates us to live in the full joy and freedom of God's grace.

1. Right Division Eliminates Confusion & Contradiction

For many Christians, the Bible can feel like a confusing and even contradictory book.

- In Genesis, God commands humanity not to eat a particular fruit; in the Gospels, Jesus says nothing that enters a man can defile him.
- In Exodus, God institutes the Sabbath as a perpetual sign; in Colossians, Paul warns against judging anyone with regard to a Sabbath day.

- In Matthew, Jesus tells His disciples to go only to the "lost sheep of the house of Israel." In Acts, He tells them to go "unto the uttermost part of the earth."
- In Romans, Paul says we are justified by faith alone; in James, we are told that faith without works is dead and cannot save.

Without the tool of right division, these passages can seem hopelessly at odds with one another, leading a believer to doubt the Bible's consistency or to simply give up on understanding difficult texts. But once a workman learns to ask "Who is being spoken to?" and "When was this spoken?" apparent contradictions dissolve into a beautiful and consistent harmony. For example, we come to understand that:

- The command about the fruit was given to Adam in the Dispensation of Innocence.
- The Sabbath was a sign for Israel under the Law.
- The command in Matthew 10 was for a specific mission before the cross; the Great Commission is for the Church Age.
- Paul is talking about our justification before God; James is talking about the evidence of our justification before men.

There are no contradictions—only God's progressive revelation unfolding through different dispensations. Right division is the key that makes the Bible fit together perfectly, from Genesis to Revelation.

2. Right Division Clarifies Our Identity, Calling & Hope

Perhaps the most liberating result of right division is a clear understanding of who we are as members of the Church, the Body of Christ. When we fail to distinguish between Israel and the

Church, we inevitably suffer from a case of mistaken identity. We try to claim promises that were never made to us and take on burdens that were never meant for us to carry.

- Our Identity: We are not an earthly people (like Israel), but a heavenly people (the Church). Our citizenship is in heaven (Philippians 3:20). We are not a nation, but a spiritual Body composed of all believers.
- Our Calling: Our mission in this age is not to establish a political kingdom on earth. That is Christ's work when He returns. Our calling is to be ambassadors for Christ (2 Corinthians 5:20), proclaiming the gospel of grace and inviting sinners to be reconciled to God through Jesus.
- Our Hope: Our "blessed hope" is not the Second Coming of Christ to the earth, but the Rapture, when Christ comes for His Church in the air (Titus 2:13; 1 Thessalonians 4:16-17). We are not looking for the Antichrist; we are looking for Jesus Christ. We are not appointed to wrath but to obtain salvation through our Lord (1 Thessalonians 5:9).

This clarity frees us from the confusion of trying to apply Israel's earthly, political program to the Church's heavenly, spiritual calling. It focuses our energy on the mission God has actually given us in this present dispensation of grace.

3. Right Division Liberates Us from Bondage of the Law

One of the most damaging consequences of failing to rightly divide is the mixing of Law and Grace. When churches place believers back under the Law — requiring them to keep the Sabbath, tithe, or follow other Old Covenant regulations—they are placing a "yoke of bondage" upon them. Scripture tells that Christ has died to set us free.

- Right division teaches us that the Law was given to Israel, not the Church.

- Right division teaches us that we are "not under the law, but under grace" (Romans 6:14).
- Right division teaches us that our motivation for holy living is not the external fear of punishment under the Law, but the internal love we have for Christ and the empowerment of the indwelling Holy Spirit.
- Right division teaches us to, "Stand fast therefore in the liberty by which Christ has made us free, and do not be entangled again with a yoke of bondage [law]." (Galatians 5:1)

Such liberty should not lead to lawlessness. It should lead to a higher and more powerful form of righteousness. Instead of trying to please God through our own fleshly efforts, which always fail, we learn to rest in the finished work of Christ and allow the Spirit to produce His fruit through us. This is the difference between a life of anxious striving and a life of joyful, grace-empowered service .

4. Right Division Magnifies the Glory of God

Ultimately, the goal of all Bible study is to see God more clearly and to worship Him more fully. Rightly dividing the Word achieves this by revealing the breathtaking scope and perfect consistency of God's sovereign plan. When we see how each dispensation demonstrates human failure and magnifies God's grace, how each covenant builds upon the last, and how all of history is moving toward the glorious enthronement of Jesus Christ on earth, our hearts are filled with awe.

We see a God who is in absolute control, who makes unconditional promises and keeps them, whose wisdom is unsearchable, whose love is unbounded, whose mercy is unending, and whose grace is truly amazing. A dispensational understanding of the Bible allows us to appreciate the distinct roles of the Father, the Son, and the Holy Spirit throughout history. It protects the integrity of God's promises to Israel, assuring us that He has not cast them away. It reveals the unique glory of the Church as the Body and Bride of Christ, and the family of God. In short, it allows us to see the whole counsel of God in all its multifaceted splendor.

Being a workman who "needeth not to be ashamed" is about more than just getting the details right. It is about handling the Word of God with such care, precision, and reverence that the character of its divine Author is put on glorious display. That is why it matters.

Chapter 10

A Workman's Summary—
A Final Review

We have now journeyed through the foundational principles of rightly dividing the Word of Truth. We have seen that the Bible is not a flat, monolithic book, but a progressive revelation of God's unchanging character and His unfolding plan for the ages. We have learned to make the critical distinctions between different dispensations, covenants, peoples, and programs. The goal of all this is not to win theological debates or to puff ourselves up with knowledge, but to become what Paul commanded Timothy to be: "a workman that needeth not to be ashamed, rightly dividing the word of truth" (2 Timothy 2:15).

This final chapter will serve as a practical summary and a simple, repeatable checklist that you can apply every time you open your Bible. By internalizing this method and consistently using it, you will transform your Bible study from a confusing exercise into a rewarding discovery of God's truth. You will move from being a passive reader of words to an active and skilled workman with understanding, confidently handling the precious truths God has revealed.

The Workman's Essential Toolkit

As we have discussed, at the heart of rightly dividing are five simple, investigative questions. Just as a carpenter has essential tools, like a hammer, saw, and measuring tape, the student of the Word has the tools of the five questions. Ask them every time you approach a passage, and they will protect you from the most common interpretive errors.

1.Who is speaking, and to whom is it spoken? This is the first and most crucial question.

2. What is being communicated? Is it a timeless principle that reveals God's character? Is it a temporary precept for a specific group? Or is it a specific promise made to a particular people?

3. When was it spoken? Situating the passage in its proper dispensation is the next vital step.

4. Where was it spoken? Understanding the geographical and cultural setting adds depth and color to the text.

5. Why was it spoken? Finally, seek to understand the author's primary purpose. What was the main point God was communicating to the original audience?

A Final Case Study: The Rich Young Ruler (Mark 10:17-22)

Let's apply our toolkit one last time to a familiar but often misunderstood passage. A rich young ruler comes to Jesus and asks, "Good Master, what shall I do that I may inherit eternal life?" Jesus responds by telling him to keep the commandments. The young man claims to have done so, and Jesus, looking at him with love, says, "One thing thou lackest: go thy way, sell whatsoever thou hast, and give to the poor, and thou shalt have treasure in heaven: and come, take up the cross, and follow me."

A person who does not rightly divide might read this and conclude that salvation requires selling all possessions, or that keeping the Law is a pathway to eternal life. But a skilled workman asks the right questions:

- **Who and To Whom?** Jesus, a minister to the "circumcision" (Romans 15:8) is speaking to a young Jewish man.

- **What?** Jesus is not presenting a universal formula for salvation (salvation is not by works). He is using the man's own chosen ground—the Law—to show him his failure.

- **When?** This occurs during Jesus' earthly ministry, under the Dispensation of Law, and before His death and resurrection inaugurated the New Covenant. The gospel of New Covenant grace was not yet preached.

- **Where?** The Bible only says that Jesus "was going out on the road," so He was traveling, likely toward Jerusalem, when the rich young ruler approached Him and asked his question.

- **Why?** By pointing to the first and greatest commandment ("Thou shalt love the Lord thy God with all thy heart... and thy neighbour as thyself") Jesus exposed the man's true idol: his wealth. The man's refusal to part with his riches proved that he had not kept the Law perfectly. Jesus used the Law exactly as it was intended: as a "schoolmaster" to reveal sin and show the man his need for a righteousness he could not produce on his own.

The application for us today is not that we must sell everything we own to be saved. The application is that anything we place before Christ is an idol, and that self-righteousness is a dead-end street. Salvation comes not by doing, but by trusting in the One who has done it all. Right division makes this clear..

The Unashamed Workman

The path to becoming a confident student of the Bible is not short, but it is deeply rewarding. It requires diligence, humility, and a consistent application of these foundational principles. As you learn to make the proper distinctions—between Israel and the Church, Law and Grace, prophecy and mystery, earth and heaven—the pieces of the biblical puzzle will begin to fit together with stunning precision.

You will stand amazed at the wisdom, consistency, and faithfulness of God. Your love for God's Word will grow, your confidence in God's truth will deepen, and your ability to share God's Word and your faith with others will be sharpened. You will be equipped to stand firm against the winds of false doctrine and to give an answer for the hope that is in you (1 Peter 3:15).

May God bless you as you "study to show thyself approved unto God, a workman that needeth not to be ashamed, rightly dividing the word of truth." (2 Timothy 2:15)

Summary

Principles of Rightly Dividing

Take a few minutes to carefully review this summary of eight principles that will help you read the Bible faithfully, interpret the verses and passages rightly, and apply God's words skillfully.

1. A text taken out of context becomes a pretext for believing whatever we want.

Faithful interpretation and application of God's Word require careful attention to context. Without it, we risk turning the living Word into a mirror that merely reflects our own desires and assumptions, becoming a pretext for believing whatever we want and validating our preferences. Mishandled Scripture may still sound biblical while quietly leading hearts away from the Lord who spoke it. This danger naturally leads to a second concern: what happens when such mishandling shapes our teaching.

2. When we rip verses from their context, we risk preaching our opinions instead of God's Word.

Out of context, the words remain biblical, but the authority has subtly shifted from God to the teacher. Instead of standing under Scripture, we stand over it, selecting and arranging verses to support our preferred conclusions. This is why context serves as a spiritual safeguard: it compels us to hear what God actually said before we decide what we think. Once context is ignored, almost any idea can be clothed in religious language and justified with a handful of disconnected verses. To avoid this, we must begin with a foundational interpretive principle.

3. The Bible cannot mean today what it never meant to its original audience.

This foundational principle anchors responsible interpretation. God spoke into real history, to real people, in real circumstances. Before we ask, "What does this mean for me?" we must ask, "What did this mean for them?" Only then are we ready to bridge from the ancient world to our present lives with biblical integrity. Honoring the original audience is not a barrier to application; it is the very path to faithful application. When we embrace this, we recognize why context is not a side issue but rather essential protection.

4. Context is not an optional extra in Bible study; it is the guardrail that keeps us from error.

Guardrails do not restrict joy; they preserve life. In the same way, attention to context protects us from misusing familiar verses as weapons, charms, or slogans. It keeps us from building doctrines on half-sentences, ignoring the flow of an argument, or overlooking the balance of the whole counsel of God. Far from making Scripture less accessible, context opens it up, helping us see connections, emphases, and themes that a surface reading might miss. And because doctrine grows out of how we read Scripture, the next principle naturally follows.

5. Right doctrine begins with right handling of Scripture; wrong handling begins with ignoring context

Sound biblical theology emerges from the way we read and connect biblical texts. Right understanding and faithful application grow out of careful observation, patient listening, and a commitment to let clearer passages shed light on more difficult ones, all within their proper historical and grammatical contexts. Conversely, when context is neglected, our theology easily drifts. That drift does not stay abstract; it directly affects how we represent God Himself.

6. We misrepresent God when we make His words serve our agenda instead of submitting our agenda to His words.

Every believer—pastors, Bible teachers, writers, and readers—faces a choice: will Scripture sit in judgment on our thinking, or will our thinking sit in judgment on Scripture? When we cherry-pick verses to reinforce what we already believe, we use the Bible rather than obey it. The call of discipleship is to bring our assumptions, emotions, and cultural loyalties under the searching light of God's revelation. True submission often requires letting Scripture contradict us, unsettle us, and reshape what we thought could never change. If we resist this, a subtle but serious heart-shift begins.

7. If we twist the Word of God, it is not Scripture that changes, but our own hearts that drift from the truth.

God's Word remains firm, but our perception of it becomes distorted when we twist verses to fit our fears, ambitions, or cultural pressures. Over time, the authority of Scripture is not only diminished but sometimes effectively denied. We begin to read past hard sayings, reframe clear commands, and downplay uncomfortable truths. The result is not a purer understanding of God's Word, but a loss of it. In contrast, there is a better, God-honoring way to approach Scripture.

8. Loving the God of the Word means we refuse to use His Word to say what He never said.

Genuine devotion does not separate love for God from loyalty to the meaning of His message. Careless handling of Scripture is not merely a stylistic issue; it is a relational one. When we selectively quote God, we effectively place words in His mouth. Those who truly love Him seek to represent Him accurately, even when His Word cuts across our preferences, challenges our traditions, or corrects long-held opinions. Reverence expresses itself in careful reading, humble listening, and a willing heart to be corrected.

For all Christians, biblical faithfulness is not a luxury—it is a moral and spiritual responsibility. God has given us a Book that reveals His works from the beginning of time and His purposes for what is yet to come. Faithfully studying the Bible and sharing God's words are expressions of a love for His truth, a humility before His authority, and a genuine care for the souls who hear. When we honor context, we are not merely practicing good study habits; we are honoring God Himself. He chose to reveal His character and will in particular words, in particular settings, at particular times, and for the good of people in every generation.

Epilogue

The Workman's Continuing Journey

Our journey through the foundational principles of rightly dividing the Word of Truth has now come to a close, but the true work is just beginning. As we have seen, the Bible is not a book to be mastered in a single reading. Think of the Bible as a lifelong companion to be studied, cherished, and applied with ever-increasing skill and reverence.

The goal of this book on rightly dividing is not to provide every answer, but to equip you with the right questions—and give you a reliable toolkit and a useful framework for your personal study.

Step out now as a workman on a path of continual growth. Journey from confusion to clarity, from anxiety to assurance, from the bondage of religious performance to the liberty of grace-empowered living. See the Bible as a majestic mountain range of divine revelation, with distinct peaks of prophecy, deep valleys of mystery, and a clear, shining path that leads always to the person and work of Jesus Christ.

As you close this book, open the pages of Scripture and remember the heart of the matter—to know God better and to love Him more. The Bible, rightly understood, will increase your awe of God, His Person and His works, and fill you with the joy of your salvation.

The Bible tells the story of a God who is faithful, even when His people are not; a Savior who fulfilled every demand of the Law, which we could not; and the Holy Spirit, who indwells, seals, and empowers us to live in victory. And the Bible promises a future of unimaginable glory, when Christ will return to reign and God will be all in all.

This is the story you are now equipped to explore with clearer vision and a confident heart. Take up your tools. Be diligent. Ask the questions. Let Scripture interpret Scripture. Lean not on your own understanding, but on the guidance of the Holy Spirit, the divine Author who is with you always and promises to guide you into all truth.

The world is full of confusion, and the Church is not immune to it. Now more than ever, there is a desperate need for believers who know what they believe and why they believe it—believers who can stand firm on the solid rock of God's Word. May you be a workman, not just a reader—A workman who handles the Word with integrity; A workman who lives in the joy of God's grace; A workman who "needeth not to be ashamed, rightly dividing the word of truth." And finally, an ambassador who shares the love of God, the saving grace of Jesus, and the sanctifying grace of the Holy Spirit with all people.

Your journey is just beginning. May it be a lifelong adventure of discovering the unsearchable riches of Christ on every page of His perfect and precious Word.

Appendix

THE KINGDOM OF GOD

The kingdom of God is not meat and drink; but righteousness, and peace, and joy in the Holy Ghost. (Rom 14:17)

Kingdom of Heaven

Physical Kingdom

"At hand"(near) during Jesus' earthy ministry.

In Heaven during the church age.

~~~

Physical Kingdom

On earth during the Millennium.

In Jerusalem. Jesus is King.

Jesus will sit on the Throne of David in the Millennial Temple

Inhabitants are subjects/citizens under the reign of Christ

Israel's role will be the lead nation with Christ's Law written in their hearts and minds (Jeremiah 31:33)

Satan bound for 1000 years.

Citizens not sealed in the Spirit.

Citizens will live by their faith in the One who sits on the throne (demonstrated by their loyalty and obedience)

KINGDOM OF GOD

A Spiritual Kingdom

KINGDOM OF HEAVEN

A physical kingdom where God dwells.

BODY OF CHRIST

All true, church-age believers who have trusted in Jesus and been born again

Kingdom of God

Spiritual Kingdom

During the Church Age

Jesus is "Head of the Body"

Church-age believers are sealed with the indwelling Holy Spirit (Eph 4:30)

And are members/parts of the body (1 Cor 12:27) with citizenship in Heaven (Phil 3:20).

We are "one" with Christ (Husband/Bride, Eph 5:25-27, 2 Cor 11:2) and joint heirs with Him (Rom 8:17)

~~~

The Body of Christ

During the Millennium

In the kingdom, the Church will rule and reign with Christ in glorified bodies (1 Cor 15:51-57)

The Kingdom of Heaven on Earth

The earthly kingdom is a "mystery" promised in the Abrahamic and David covenants, foreshadowed in Abraham's faith, revealed as a coming kingdom by Paul, and guaranteed by God—because God is faithful to keep and fulfill all His promises.

Let us hold fast the profession of our faith without wavering; (for he is faithful that promised) Heb 10:23

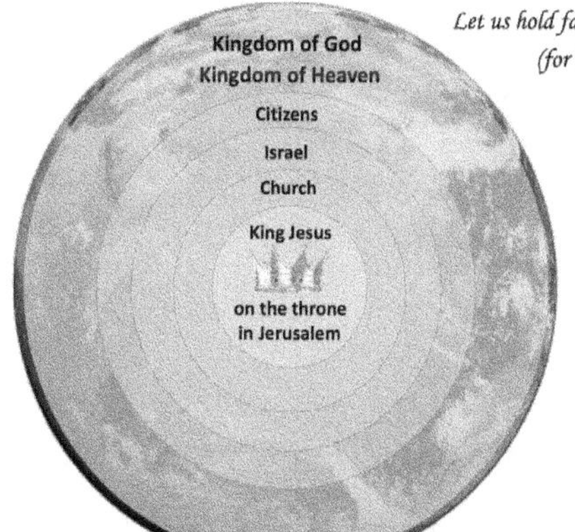

For the earth shall be filled with the knowledge of the glory of the LORD, as the waters cover the sea.
Hab 2:14

For a color PDF of the chart, email hope@reasonsforhopeJesus.com. Specify "Kingdom Chart" in your email.

For a PDF of the chart,
email hope@reasonsforhopeJesus.com.
Specify "Mosaic Law & Royal Law Chart."

THE MOSAIC LAW & THE ROYAL LAW

EXODUS 12 JAMES 2:8

LOVE GOD

HONOR PARENTS
NO MURDER, NO ADULTERY

JESUS
Sabbath rest in Christ

NO STEALING, NO LYING
NO COVETING

NO OTHER GODS
NO IDOLS
HONOR HIS NAME

**The Mosaic Law gave rules.
The Royal Law gives love.**

**The Mosaic Law condemns.
The Royal Law gives life.**

**The Mosaic Law was written on stone tablets.
The Royal Law is written on hearts by the Spirit.**

**The Mosaic Law exposes our need for a Savior.
The Royal Law flows from t he Savior who fulfilled the law and reigns as King.**

Jesus summed up the first three commandments as being our vertical relationship with God: "Love the Lord your God..."

Jesus summed up the last six commandments as being our horizontal relationship with others: "Love your neighbor as yourself."

Matthew 22:37-40

The fourth commandment is the Sabbath rest. In Jesus, we find rest.

Matthew 11:28, Hebrerws 4:9-11

The Vertical	The Horizontal
Our relationship with God	Our relationship with man
The indicative (what God has done for us)	The imperative (what we should do for others)
Positional standing	Practical living
Love flowing from God to us	Love flowing from us to others
Connecting us to God in Heaven	Sending us out in the world, from East to West
Reminding us to look up	Reminding us to look around

John 13:34-5 A new commandment I give unto you, That you love one another; as I have loved you, that you also love one another. By this shall all men know that you are my disciples, if you have love one to another.

For a PDF of the chart,
email hope@reasonsforhopeJesus.com.
Specify "Eight Dispensations Chart."

The Eight Dispensations

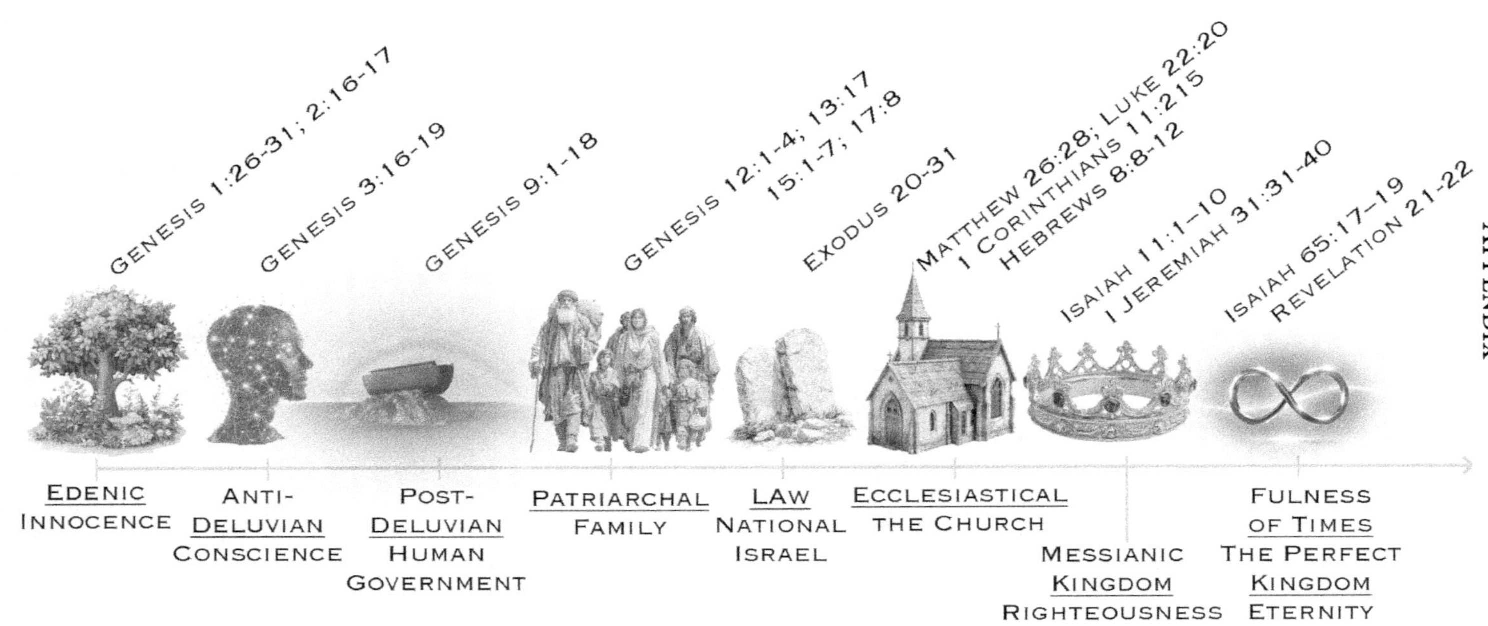

For a PDF of the chart,
email hope@reasonsforhopeJesus.com.
Specify "Abrahamic/New Covenant Chart."

THE ABRAHAMIC COVENANT POINTED TO THE NEW AND BETTER COVENANT IN CHRIST

HEBREWS 8:7. FOR IF THAT FIRST COVENANT HAD BEEN FAULTLESS, THEN NO PLACE WOULD HAVE BEEN SOUGHT FOR A SECOND. IN THAT HE SAYS, "A NEW COVENANT," HE HAS MADE THE FIRST OBSOLETE...

ABRAHAMIC COVENANT	**NEW COVENANT**
• A heifer, goat, ram, turtledove and pigeon for sin offerings (Lev 1).	• Jesus' body — an offering for sin (Ro 8:3, Eph 5:20).
• The heifer, goat, and ram were cut, broken (Lev 1:6,12, Gen 15:9-11).	• Jesus' body was cut (John 19:1) and b ken (1 Cor 11:24).
• The turtledove and pigeon were not cut (Lev 1:17).	• No bones broken (Ex 12:43,46, Num 9:12, Ps 34:20, John 19:31-33).
• The animals and the birds were laid out on the earth (Gen 5:10).	• Jesus was raised up on a cross: sunke into the earth (Mk 15:25).
• Animal's bodies separated (Gen 15:10)	• Jesus was forsaken (Mat 27:46).
• Darkness upon the land (Gen 15:17).	• Darkness upon the land (Matt 27:45).
• God alone walked between the animals as fire and light (Gen 15:12,17).	• God alone judged the sins of the worl that Jesus bore (Isa 53:4, 1 Pet 2:24).
• Fire consumed the sacrifices (Lev 9:24	• God is a consuming fire (Heb 9:29).
• God required the blood of circumcision for man to enter into the Abrahamic Covenant (Gen 17:10-14).	• By the blood of Jesus man is able to e ter into the New Covenant (Matt 26:28 Cor 11:25, Rom 5:9, Eph 1:7).
• Circumcision is the sign of the Abrahamic Covenant (Gen 17:11).	• Jesus' blood is the sign of the New Co enant (Mk 14:24, Lk 22:20, 1 Cor 11:25
• Circumcision was of the flesh, done by the hand of man (Gen 17:11).	• Circumcision of the heart; God's worl without hands (Rom 2:29, Col 2:11).
• Man made a choice by faith to be circumcised in the flesh.	• Man makes a choice by faith to come to Jesus; and is then circumcised in the heart.

For a color PDF of the chart,
email hope@reasonsforhopeJesus.com.
Specify “70 Weeks of Daniel Chart.”

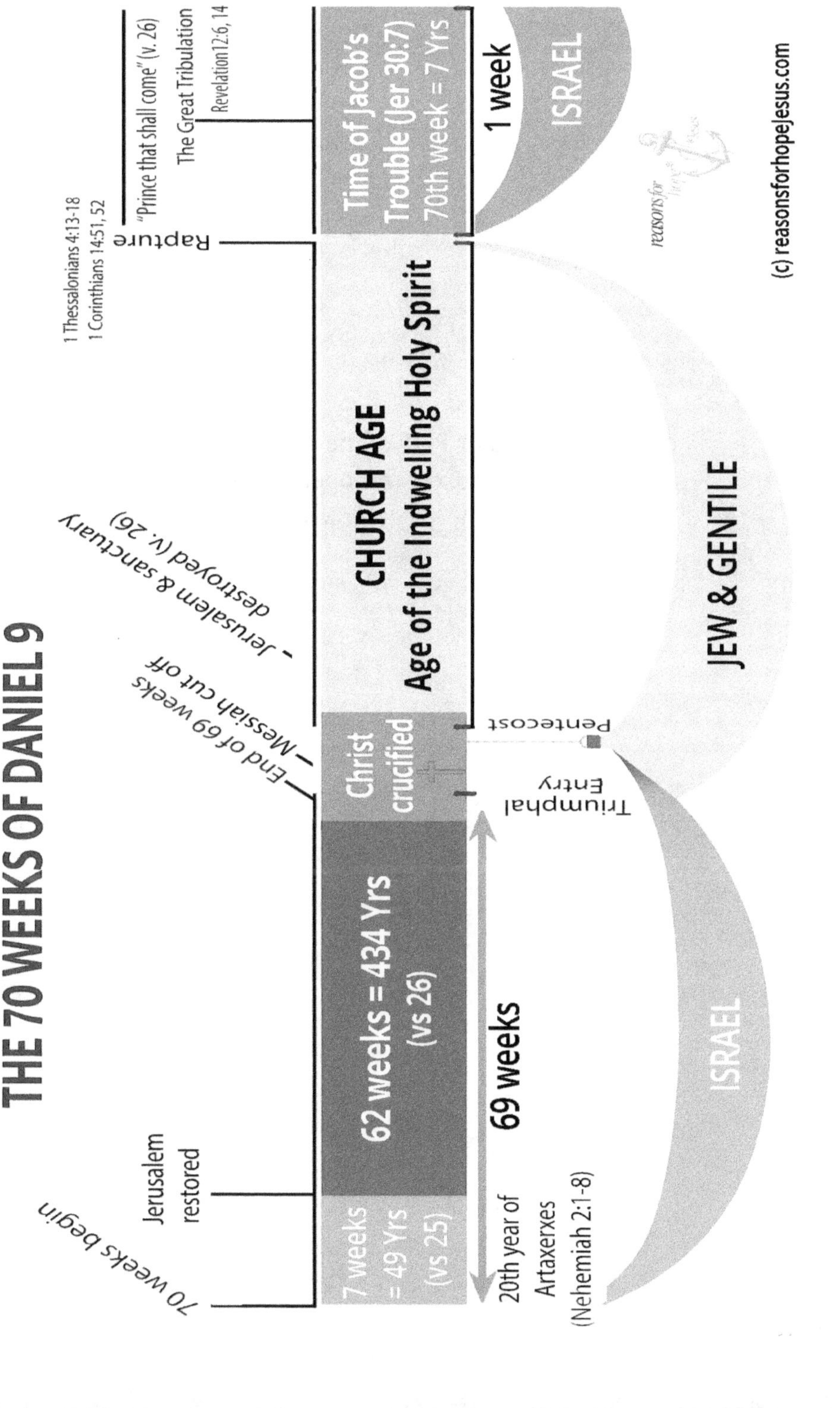

THE 70 WEEKS OF DANIEL 9

70 weeks begin

Jerusalem restored

End of 69 weeks

Messiah cut off

Jerusalem & sanctuary destroyed (v. 26)

1 Thessalonians 4:13-18
1 Corinthians 14:51, 52

Rapture

"Prince that shall come" (v. 26)

The Great Tribulation

Revelation12:6, 14

7 weeks = 49 Yrs (vs 25)

62 weeks = 434 Yrs (vs 26)

Christ crucified

CHURCH AGE
Age of the Indwelling Holy Spirit

Time of Jacob's Trouble (Jer 30:7)
70th week = 7 Yrs

69 weeks

20th year of Artaxerxes (Nehemiah 2:1-8)

Triumphal Entry

Pentecost

1 week

ISRAEL

JEW & GENTILE

ISRAEL

reasons for hope Jesus

For a color PDF of the chart,
email hope@reasonsforhopeJesus.com.
Specify "Rightly Dividing Chart."

Rightly Dividing the Word of Truth

(2 Timothy 2:15)

Creation & Fall

God creates; man falls

promise of a Savior

Promise to Abraham

God gives Law; reveals sin and need for a perfect sacrifice

God chooses a people; promises blessing through Abraham's Seed

Cross & Resurrection

God provides the perfect sacrifice – Jesus

Church Age

God forms the Body of Christ

Gospel to all nations

Future Fulfillment

God fulfills all promises; restores all things

Rightly Dividing = Cutting a Straight Path

- See the whole road, not just one verse
- Honor the differences God built into His plan
- Keep Christ and the cross at the center

Always by grace through faith – one plan, many stages, all centered on Christ

For a color PDF of the chart,
email hope@reasonsforhopeJesus.com.
Specify "Rightly Dividing NT Books Chart"

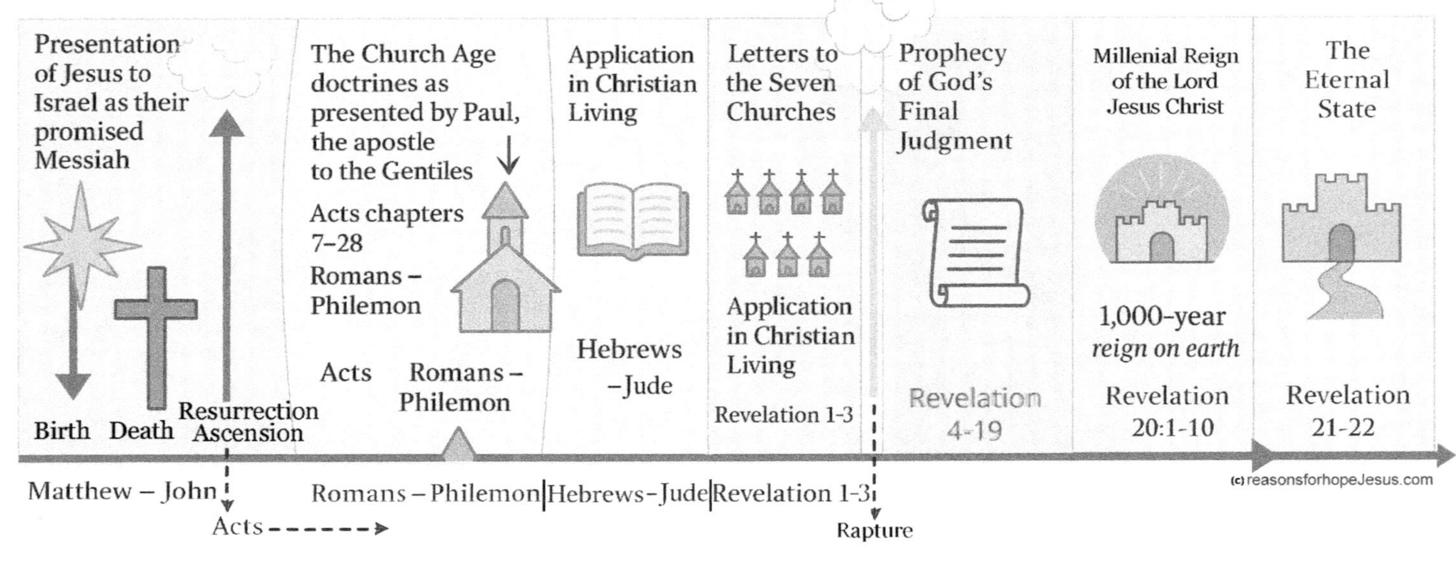
The Books of the New Testament – Rightly Divided for Right Handling
Presentation of Jesus to Israel as their promised Messiah
Birth
Death
Resurrection
Ascension
The Church Age doctrines as presented by Paul, the apostle to the Gentiles
Acts chapters 7–28
Romans – Philemon
Acts
Romans – Philemon
Application in Christian Living
Hebrews –Jude
Letters to the Seven Churches
Application in Christian Living
Revelation 1-3
Prophecy of God's Final Judgment
Revelation 4-19
Millenial Reign of the Lord Jesus Christ
1,000-year *reign on earth*
Revelation 20:1-10
The Eternal State
Revelation 21-22
Matthew – John
Romans – Philemon
Hebrews–Jude
Revelation 1-3
Acts
Rapture
(c) reasonsforhopeJesus.com

Books & Resources from this Author

Who Said That? Common Everyday Sayings
This is a great book to give to unbelievers. It's simply a look at everyday sayings originating from God's Word. At the end of the book is a gospel presentation.

A Room with a View of Eternity—
The Last Will & Testament of the Lord Jesus Christ
Take a seat at the Master's table. Learn about the Lord's final words to His faithful disciples (John 13-17), and the riches He gives to all who are His. This book will bless and encourage you, provide you with hope, and help you live in the joy of your salvation.

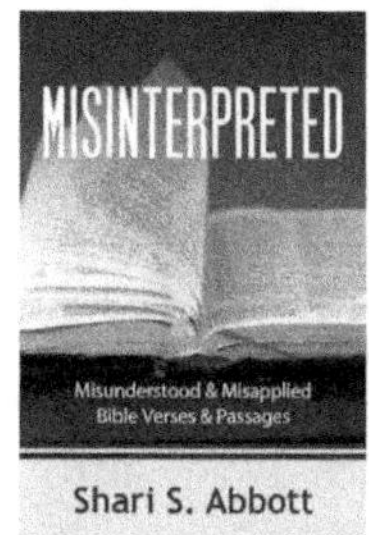

MISINTERPRETED - Misunderstood & Misapplied Bible Verses & Passages—Sometimes Scripture is wrongly taught with an intention to deceive, but most often it is unintentional. As Christians, we must be diligent in discerning truth —God's truth from His Word.

Got Questions? We have Reasons for Hope
Reasons Books 1, 2, 3 & 4

Real questions from real people. Each book has 30 questions and 30 answers with reasons for hope.

Why the Butterfly? Rightly Remembering Jesus—This book isn't about butterflies. . .it's all about Jesus! Discover how rightly remembering will establish your heart, anchor your soul, and transform your mind. A quick read that will give you a heavenly perspective on this journey we call life!

Remember Me - A Course About Rightly Remembering Seven video study sessions that teach rightly remembering and will ignite in you a desire to filter everything you think, say and do through the hope that is found in Jesus Christ. Learn how *rightly remembering* will establish your heart, anchor your soul, and transform your mind.

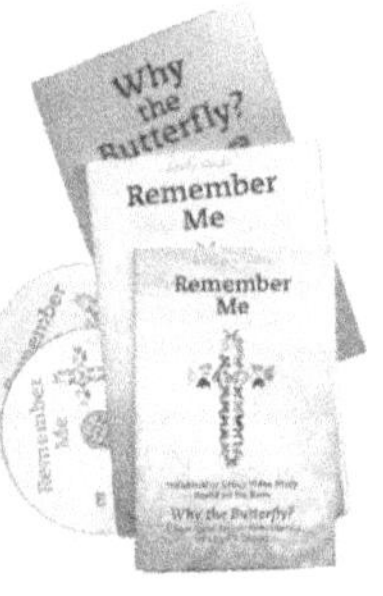

Fun with Shuns Learn the key doctrines of the Christian faith by understanding the many words in the Bible that end in "-tion". The study includes five short videos. If you can't fully explain why you believe what you believe, then you need this study. DVD and book for group or individual study.

Hear, See, Speak No Evil—Plus a Fourth Monkey The three little monkeys, with their proverbial quip, "Hear No Evil, See No Evil, and Speak No Evil," date back as far as 17th century. What biblical lessons do these monkeys offer? And what about the newest warning. . .post no evil?

How to Witness to Jehovah's Witnesses~ Apologetics Answers & Verses Get prepared to defend what you believe and be able to present biblical truth the next time a Jehovah's Witness comes to your door. Don't be out-witnessed by a Jehovah's Witness.

Quotable Quotes - Words Worth Remembering is a treasury of timeless wisdom from Christian voices across the ages. Carefully chosen quotations are paired with Scripture references to encourage you to delve deeper into the biblical truths that relate to the insightful quotes—as a way to draw closer to the heart of God.

Forty Names of Jesus for Forty Days of Lent — A devotional book with short daily readings to inspire your mind and deepen your love for "The Risen Christ," your Shepherd, Savior, and King. When the forty days are complete, continue by exploring more names and titles of Jesus.

Rightly Dividing the Word of Truth — With simple explanations and Scripture-centered teaching, this book will help you discover how a right understanding of Scripture brings clarity instead of confusion, confidence instead of doubt, and joy as you see how every part of the Bible fits together in God's perfect plan.

Visit www.reasonsforhopeJesus.com/store

Have Hope!

Now hope does not disappoint, because the love of God has been poured out in our hearts by the Holy Spirit who was given to us.

—Romans 5:5

Be Bold!

Therefore, since we have such hope, we use great boldness of speech;

—2 Corinthians 3:12

[Praying] for me, that utterance may be given to me, that I may open my mouth boldly to make known the mystery of the gospel, for which I am an ambassador in chains; that in it I may speak boldly, as I ought to speak.

—Ephesians 6:19-20

This hope we have as an anchor for the soul, both sure and steadfast. (Hebrews 6:19)

Helping Christians to know Jesus better, by

Offering biblical answers and reasoning from God's Word, and

Promoting the benefits and joys of spending time with God in prayer and in reading and studying His Word, which leads to

Enjoying God, finding rest in Jesus, and living to honor Him and serve others.

Get *equipped* with KNOWLEDGE! ✝

Be *encouraged* in HOPE! ⚓

Live *empowered* with LOVE! ♥

About Reasons for Hope* Jesus

Our ministry exists to glorify God by equipping Christians with biblical knowledge, understanding, and wisdom. Knowing and trusting God and growing in understanding of His will and ways will change our world. Jesus is the Reason this Ministry Exists, but YOU make it possible!

If Reasons for Hope* Jesus has blessed you, please consider supporting our ministry. Your goodwill and generosity makes possible our mission to equip, encourage, and empower the body of Christ and reach the lost with the gospel of saving grace. www.reasonsforhopeJesus.com/donate.

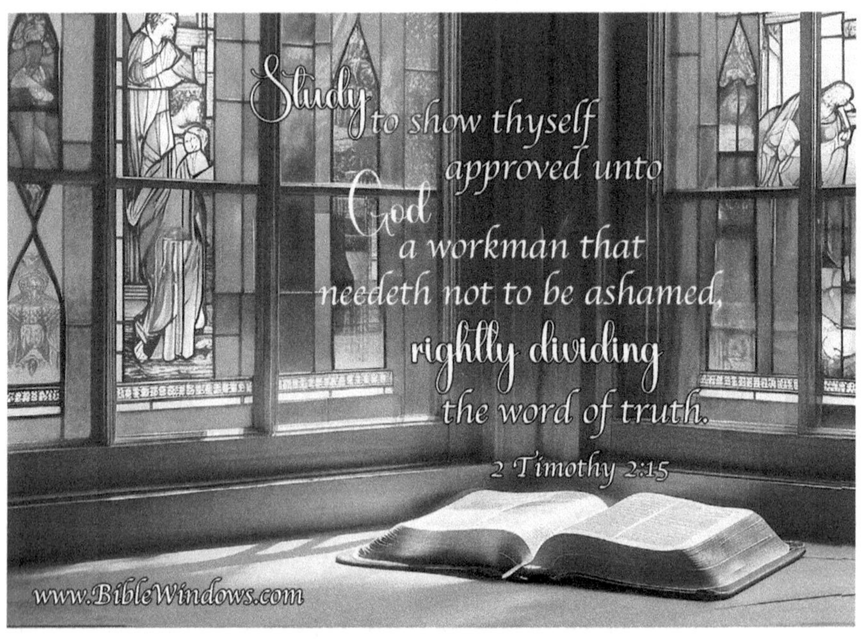

Visit www.BibleWindows.com
for all our song videos and
Bible teachings videos

Questions?

Email us at questions@reasonsforhopeJesus.com

Contact Us

Email us at hope@reasonsforhopeJesus.com

Connect With Us

www.reasonsforhopeJesus.com

www.biblewindows.com

Facebook: www.facebook.com/reasonsforhopeJesus/

Twitter: www.twitter.com/reasons4hope

YouTube: www.youtube.com/reasonsforhopeJesus

Visit the Store

www.reasonsforhopeJesus.com/store

Sign Up

At www.reasonsforhopeJesus.com for apologetics teachings and biblical encouragement with true hope and real joy.

May the God of hope fill you with all joy and peace in believing, that you may abound in hope by the power of the Holy Spirit. Romans 15:13

Christ is the sum of the whole Bible—prophesied, typified, prefigured, exhibited, demonstrated—to be found in every leaf, almost in every line. The Scriptures being but as it were, the swaddling bands of the child Jesus.

— Thomas Adams (1583–1653)

Visit our website and watch:

JESUS IN EVERY STORY IN THE OLD TESTAMENT

reasonsforhopejesus.com/jesus-in-every-story-old-testament/

JESUS IN EVERY STORY IN THE NEW TESTAMENT

reasonsforhopejesus.com/jesus-in-every-story-new-testament/

Share the Gospel

Since we have the same spirit of faith, according to what is written, "I believed and therefore I spoke," we also believe and therefore speak.

—2 Corinthians 4:13

As it is written: "How beautiful are the feet of those who preach the gospel of peace, Who bring glad tidings of good things!"

—Romans 10:15

www.ingramcontent.com/pod-product-compliance
Lightning Source LLC
LaVergne TN
LVHW020647100826
845148LV00012B/2359

* 9 7 8 1 7 3 6 1 0 7 6 5 2 *